T0284066

ENDORSEMENTS

This concise commentary can be particularly beneficial for individuals seeking to explore the Jewish roots of the Bible and gain a comprehensive understanding of its teachings. Rabbi Dr. Koelner delves into the historical, cultural, and linguistic aspects of the text, providing insights that enhance the reader's understanding of the Scriptures. I highly recommend this commentary that contributes to a more nuanced and enriched interpretation of First and Second Thessalonians.

—Ezra Golan, Pastor, Israel

It is an honor to be able to endorse the sound Biblical teaching and scholarship of Yosef Koelner. His latest writing about 1 and 2 Thessalonians will be respected by members of the theological community. Yossi has the benefits of being raised in an Orthodox Jewish home, serving as a Messianic Congregational leader for over 45 years, and teaching extensively in Latin America. He is a first-rate scholar with an MA Degree in Jewish Studies from Gratz College which is the oldest Jewish University in the United States and holds a Doctor of Practical Ministry from the Wagner Leadership Institute.

—Rabbi Paul Liberman. President-International Messianic Jewish Alliance, Past president-Messianic Jewish Alliance of America

FIRST AND SECOND
THESSALONIANS

A MESSIANIC COMMENTARY

FIRST AND SECOND
THESSALONIANS
LETTERS OF HOPE,
ENCOURAGEMENT, AND
AFFIRMATION

RABBI YOSEF KOELNER

Lederer Books
An imprint of
Messianic Jewish Publishers

Clarksville, MD 21029

Printed in the United States of America
Graphic Design by Yvonne Vermillion,
MagicGraphix.com
Editing by George Koch

ISBN: 978-1-951833-43-5

Published by
Lederer Books
A division of
Messianic Jewish Publishers
6120 Day Long Lane
Clarksville, Maryland 21029

Distributed by
Messianic Jewish Resources Int'l.
www.MessianicJewish.net
Individual and Trade Order Line: 800-410-7647
Email: lederer@messianicjewish.net

Author's Note: The following is not a verse-by-verse commentary. Its purpose is to bring to light Jewish concepts in selected passages that enhance one's understanding of the text.

"One can survive for a while without food, but not without hope."

Mala Kacenberg, *Mala's Cat* – A Memoir of Survival in World War II [1]

---

1. Mala Kacenberg, *Mala's Cat* (New York: Pegasus, 2022), 101.

Dedicated to Harold and Dorothy Tobiansky
of blessed memory, my foster parents who took a discouraged
teenage orphan into their home. And with unconditional love and
encouragement restored to him a hope for the future.

TABLE OF CONTENTS

GENERAL EDITOR'S PREFACE

Nearly all Bible commentators emphasize the importance of understanding the historical, cultural, and grammatical aspects of any text of Scripture. As has been said, "A text without a context is a pretext." In other words, to assume one can understand what God has revealed through those who present his Word—prophets, poets, visionaries, apostles—without knowing the context is presumption. To really understand God's Word, it is essential to know something about who wrote it, to whom, what was said, what it originally meant, and when, where, and why it was written.

By now, everyone knows the New Testament is a thoroughly Jewish book, written entirely by Jews, taking place in and around Israel. The people written about—Yeshua (Jesus), Paul, Peter, James, John, etc.—were all Jews who never abandoned their identities or people. The topics covered—sin, salvation, resurrection, Torah, Sabbath, how to "walk with God," the Millennium, etc.—were all Jewish topics that came from the Hebrew Scripture. Many expressions were Jewish idioms of that day. So, to fully understand the New Testament, it must be viewed through "Jewish eyes."

There are commentaries for women, men, teens, even children. There are commentaries that focus on financial issues in the Bible. Others provide archaeological material. Some commentaries are topical. Others are the works of eminent men and women of God. Yet, no commentary series has focused on the Jewish context of each of the New Testament books.... until now.

Some of the world's top Messianic Jewish theologians contributed their knowledge and understanding to this series. Each has written on a book or books of the New Testament he has specialized in, making sure to present the Jewish aspects—the original context—of each book. These works are not meant to be a verse-by-verse exegetical commentary. There are many excellent ones available. The commentaries in this series focus on the Jewish aspects, often missed, along with explaining the book.

Several different authors contributed these commentaries, each in his own style. Just as the Gospels were written by four different men, each with his own perspective and style, these volumes too have variations.

You may see some actual Hebrew expressions or transliterations of Hebrew names in the New Testament. Thus, one writer might refer to the Apostle to the Gentiles as Paul. Another might write *Sha'ul*, Paul's Hebrew name. Still another might write *Saul*, an Anglicized version of *Sha'ul*. And some might write *Saul/Paul* to reflect, not reject, the different ways this servant of Messiah was known.

Another variation is the amount of reference material. Some have ample footnotes or endnotes, while others incorporate references within the text. Some do not have many notes. Some present words in their original languages, either Hebrew or Greek.

So, I invite you to put on your "Jewish glasses" and look at the New Testament in a way that may open new understanding for you, as you get to know the God of Israel and his Messiah better.

Rabbi Barry Rubin
General Editor and Publisher

First Thessalonians
Introduction

Sha'ul/Paul is the uncontested author of First Thessalonians. It is his earliest extant letter and was written from Corinth circa 50 C.E. It is obvious that his experience in Corinth served as a frame of reference for many of the concepts he expresses in this letter.

Almost immediately after its inception, the nascent community of believers in Yeshua at Thessaloniki was subjected to unrelenting opposition and persecution. They were a resilient group whose hope was that Yeshua would imminently relieve and rescue them from their distress. The day of their deliverance would occur at the time of the *parousia*, the beginning phase of the Day of the Lord.

Due to the delay of that Day, their hope was diminishing, and they began to grow discouraged and dismayed. Sha'ul wrote to the Thessalonians to restore their hope, encourage their perseverance, and clarify any misunderstandings regarding the timing and details concerning the Day of the Lord, the *Parousia*.

Sha'ul's theological perspective in respect to the Day of the Lord can be traced back to his training as an apocalyptic Pharisee as well as to revelations he received from the Lord Yeshua about that Day.

The Thessalonian correspondence is an apocalyptic theological treatise on the Day of the Lord.

SHA'UL, THE
APOCALYPTIC PHARISEE

Apocalyptic eschatology was central to Sha'ul's message[1] The appearance of the resurrected Yeshua changed Sha'ul's life, and his writings are replete with references to the Day of the Lord and the resurrection from the dead.[2]

Like many other Jews of the time—including such figures as John the Baptist and Yeshua of Nazareth—Pharisees held to a kind of apocalyptic worldview that had developed toward the very end of the biblical period and into the first century.[3]

For Sha'ul, "The Torah's sacrificial system was incapable of imparting eschatological righteousness (8:3). The answer for both Jews and gentiles is not the Torah but the *evangelion* (Good News) of Yeshua and the *pneuma* (Spirit) that he imparts."[4] Sha'ul believed he was living in the end times and that the resurrection from the dead was imminent.

Gabriele Boccacinni agrees: "Paul is heavily indebted to the apocalyptic ideology of his time because he had been an apocalyptic Diaspora Pharisee before his conversion. Apocalyptic is for Paul the bearer of prophecy in new circumstances. It keeps alive the prophetic promises about a new act of God in the future that will surpass God's acts in the past and bring about a transformed creation.

---

1. Jacob Neusner and Bruce Chilton, *In Quest of the Historical Pharisees,* 126.
2. Acts 9:1–5; 22:3–16; 26:9–18; 1 Cor. 15; Gal. 1:16; 1 Thess. 1:13–18.
3. Bart D. Ehrman, *The Triumph of Christianity: How a Forbidden Religion Swept the World*, 44.
4. Mark Kinzer, *Paul and the Torah in Apocalyptic Perspective*, Welcome to Enoch Seminar October 26, http://enochseminar.org/review/14933.

Paul must be understood within Second Temple Judaism, and specifically, with Jewish apocalyptic eschatology."[5]

Fredriksen rightly concludes that Sha'ul is a mid-first-century Jew, and a charismatic, apocalyptic visionary: it is within that context that his definitions of messiah/*Christos* must stand.[6]

---

5. Gabriele Boccaccini and Carlos A. Segovia, *Paul the Jew: Rereading the Apostle as a Figure of Second Temple Judaism*, 85.
6. Paula Fredriksen, *Paul: The Pagan's Apostle*.

THE HISTORY OF THESSALONIKI

Sha'ul and his companions visit to Thessaloniki, Macedonia circa 49 C.E. follows their customary pattern of visiting the Jewish communities of the Diaspora (Acts 17:1–10; cf. 13:5–12,13–52; 16:14; 18:4).

Two legendary names Thessaloniki is said to have borne in early times are Emathia [7] and Halia, [8] the latter referring to the town's maritime position. During the first period of its authentic history, it was known under the name of Therma, [9] derived, in common with the designation of the gulf Thermaicus Sinus, from the hot salt-springs found on various parts of this coast. [10]

Originally named Therma, Thessaloniki was founded in 315 B.C.E. by General Kassandros who married the half-sister of Alexander the Great, daughter of King Fillip the 2nd of the Macedonian Kingdom. In 168 B.C.E. Thessaloniki became part of the Roman Empire. In 146/8 B.C.E. the city became the seat of administration when Macedonia was designated a senatorial province. It received the status of a free city in 42 B.C.E. Subsequently in 44 C.E., Thessaloniki became the administrative capital of the Roman province of Macedonia. The city's commercial importance and economic power derived from its extremely favorable transportation location on the Thermaic Gulf. Strabo estimates its population to be between 65,000 and 100,000. [11]

---

7. Zonar, *Hist.* 12:26.
8. Steph. B. *s. v.*
9. θέρ μα, Esch.; θέρμη, Herod, Thucyd.; θέρ μαι, Malelas, *Chronog.* 190.
10. https://www.biblicalcyclopedia.com/T/thessalonica.html.
11. Hilary Le Cornu and Joseph Shulam, *A Commentary on the Jewish Roots of Acts*, 926.

THE HISTORY OF THE JEWISH COMMUNITY OF THESSALONIKI

The time when the Jews first settled in Thessaloniki is a question that has not yet been historically resolved. J. Nehama believed isolated seafaring Jews settled in Thessaloniki as early as the pre-exilic period circa before 600 B.C.E.[12]

Some researchers claim there were Jews in Thessaloniki at the time of its founding (315 B.C.E.).[13] It is possible these Jews were mercenaries under the command of General Kassandros, the brother-in-law of Alexander the Great and the founder of Thessaloniki/Therma. According to Josephus, who cites the work of Hecataeus here, Jewish mercenaries took part in the campaigns of Alexander the Great (Josephus, *Ap.* i.200–204). During the Hasmonean period, there was brisk exchange between Judea and Greece (1 Macc. 12:2, 7; 15:22f.; 2 Macc. 5:9; Josephus, *Ant.* xii.225; xiv.149–55).[14] It is also conjectured that many Jews who arrived in the city were from Alexandria circa 140 B.C.E.

After Alexander's death, the Jews spread rapidly in all the large cities of the provinces which had formed his empire. Hence there is no doubt that, in the 1st century of the Christian era, they were settled in considerable numbers at Thessaloniki; indeed, this

---

12. Rainer Riesner and Doug Stott, *Paul's Early Period: Chronology, Mission Strategy, Theology*, 344.
13 . "Jewish Community of Thessaloniki." *Hellenic Resources Network.* http://www.hri.org/culture97/eng/eidika_programmata/koinothtes/jewish_community.
14. Riesner and Stott, *Paul's Early Period*, 344.

circumstance contributed to the first establishment of Christianity there by Paul.[15]

There are additional reasons why some Jewish people may have settled there during the Hellenistic/Roman period. Thessaloniki had blossomed into a thriving harbor city.[16]

During those ancient times, the appeal of Hellenism was strong: Jews inhabiting Thessaloniki and surrounding regions incorporated Greek into their religious ceremonies and were known as Romaniotes.[17] Epigraphs (in Greek) on sarcophagi, circa 2nd & 3d century C.E., attest to the Jewish presence[18] as well as the column from the ancient synagogue at *Stobi*, just 100 kilometers away, with the inscription in Greek referring to *Polycharmos*, Father of the Synagogue."[19] Most interesting is a recently found inscription from the late second or early third century, only recently published *(ZPE* 102 [19941 297–306), which speaks about a synagogue that can be translated as Jewish communities or religious buildings.[20]

---

15 . "Thessalonica." *McClintock and Strong Biblical Cyclopedia.* https://www.biblicalcyclopedia.com/T/thessalonica.html.

16. A. E. Vacalopoulos, *A History of Thessalonica*, 9.

17. Paul Isaac Hagouel, "History of the Jews of Thessaloniki: from Jews to Hellenes, from Antiquity to Modern Times." International Scientific Conference – Jews: History, Tradition, Culture, Language & Religion." December 2014. https://www.academia.edu/9855342.

18. Pantelis M. Nigdelis, "Synagoge(n) und Gemeinde der Juden in Thessalonika: Fragen aufgrund einer neuen judischen Grabinschrift der Kaiserzeit," *Zeitschrift für Papyrologie und Epigraphik* 102, 297–306.

19 . N. Vulić, "Inscription grecque de Stobi," *Bulletin de Correspondance Hellénique*, Vol. 56, 291–298. https://www.persee.fr/doc/bch_0007-4217_1932_num_56_1_2840.

20. Irina Levinskaya, *The Book of Acts in Its First Century Setting*, 155.

Outline of
First Thessalonians

I.   Salutations and Blessings (1:1)
II.   Loving Words of Hope and Encouragement (1:2–10)
   A. Faith, love, hope, and power (1:2–5)
     B. Despite suffering model believers (1:6–9)
     C. Maintaining the hope of Yeshua's imminent return (1:10)
  III. The Characteristics of Their Apostleship (2:1–12)
     A. Suffering (2:1)
     B. Pure motives and approved by God (2:2–6)
     C. Hard workers whose ministry was self-funded (2:7–9)
     D. Fathers (The Apostles) who comfort their children (The Thessalonians) (2:10–12)
        1. Praise and comfort for their children being receptive to the Word of God (2:13)
        2. Endurance and perseverance during times of persecution (2:14–16)
        3. Yearning to visit their children (2:17–18)
        4. Expressions of love for their children (2:19–20)
  IV. Timothy's Visit
     A. Timothy sent to strengthen and encourage the Thessalonians because of their trials (3:1–5)
     B. Timothy's report (3:6)
     C. Sha'ul's response to Timothy's report (3:7–13)
     1. Encouragement (3:7-9)
     2. Constant prayer (3:10)
     3. Blessings (3:11–13)
  V. Personal Conduct and Further Instructions (4:1–5:22)
     A. Leading a life that is pleasing to God (4:1–2)
     B. Holiness and sexual purity (4:3–8)
     C. Brotherly love (4:9–10)
     D. Hard workers who lead a simple and peaceful life (4:11–12)
     E. The hope of the resurrection and its timing (4:13–5:11)
     F. Conduct within the faith community (5:12–22)
  VI.   Final Blessings (5:23–28)

THE TEXT OF
FIRST THESSALONIANS

1 From: Sha'ul, Sila and Timothy

To: The Messianic Community of the Thessalonians, united with God the Father and the Lord Yeshua the Messiah:

Grace to you and *shalom*.

We always thank God for all of you, regularly mentioning you in our prayers, calling to mind before God our Father what our Lord Yeshua the Messiah has brought about in you—how your trust produces action, your love hard work, and your hope perseverance. We know, brothers, that God has loved and chosen you; that the Good News we brought did not become for you a matter only of words, but also one of power, the *Ruach HaKodesh* and total conviction—just as you know how we lived for your sakes when we were with you. You, indeed, became imitators of us and of the Lord; so that even though you were going through severe troubles, you received the Word with joy from the *Ruach HaKodesh*.

Thus, you became a pattern for all the believers in Macedonia and Achaia; for the Lord's message sounded forth from you not only in Macedonia and Achaia, but everywhere your trust toward God became known. The result is that we don't need to say anything; since they themselves keep telling us about the welcome we received from you and how you turned to God from idols, to serve the true God, the one who is alive, and to wait for his Son Yeshua, whom he raised from the dead, to appear from heaven and rescue us from the impending fury of God's judgment.

2 You yourselves know, brothers, that our visit to you was not fruitless. On the contrary, although we had already suffered and been outraged in Philippi, as you know, we had the courage, united with our God, to tell you the Good News even under great pressure. For the appeal we make does not flow from error or from impure motives, neither do we try to trick people. Instead, since God has tested us and found us fit to be entrusted with Good News, this is how we speak: not to win favor with people but with God, who tests our hearts. For, as you know, never did we employ flattering talk, nor did we put on a false front to mask greed—God is witness. Nor did we seek human praise—either from you or from others. As emissaries of the Messiah, we could have made our weight felt; but instead, we were gentle when we were with you, like a mother feeding and caring for her children. We were so devoted to you that we were glad to share with you not only God's Good News but also our own lives, because you had become very dear to us. For you remember, brothers, our toil and hardship, how we worked night and day not to put a burden on any of you while we were proclaiming God's Good News to you. You are witnesses, and so is God, of how holy, righteous and blameless our behavior was in the sight of you believers; for you know that we treated each one of you the way a father treats his children—we encouraged you and comforted you and appealed to you to lead lives worthy of God, who calls you into his Kingdom and glory. Another reason we regularly thank God is that when you heard the Word of God from us, you received it not merely as a human word, but God's Word, which is at work in you believers. For, brothers, you came to be imitators of God's congregations in Y'hudah that are united with the Messiah Yeshua— you suffered the same things from your countrymen as they did from the Judeans who both killed the Lord Yeshua and the prophets and chased us out too. They are displeasing God and opposing all mankind by trying to keep us from speaking to the Gentiles, so that they may be delivered. Their object seems to be always to make their sins as bad as possible! But God's fury will catch up with them in the end. And as for us, brothers, when we were deprived of your company for a brief time—in person, but not in thought—we missed you and tried hard to see you. We wanted so much to come to you— I, Sha'ul, tried more than once—but the Adversary stopped us. For when our Lord Yeshua returns, what will be our hope, our joy, our crown to boast about? Won't it be you? Yes, you are our glory and our joy!

3 So when we could no longer stand it, we agreed to be left in Athens alone and sent Timothy, our brother and God's fellow worker for the Good News of the Messiah, to make you solid and encourage you in your trust; so that none of you would let these persecutions unsettle him. For you yourselves know that these are bound to come to us; even when we were with you, we kept telling you in advance that we were about to be persecuted; and indeed, it has happened, as you know. That is the reason, after I could stand it no longer, I sent to find out about your trust. I was afraid that somehow the Tempter had tempted you, and our hard work had been wasted.

But now Timothy has come to us from you, bringing good news about your trust and love, and telling us that you remember us well and are always longing to see us, just as we long to see you. Because of this, brothers, despite all our trouble and distress, we were comforted over you—because of your trust; so that now we are alive; since you continue to stand fast, united with the Lord.

Indeed, how can we thank God enough for you or express to our God all the joy we feel because of you? Night and day we pray as hard as we can that we will be able to see you face to face and supply whatever shortcomings there may be in your trust. May God our Father and our Lord Yeshua direct our way to you.

And as for you, may the Lord make you increase and overflow in love toward each other, indeed, toward everyone, just as we do toward you; so that he may give you the inner strength to be blameless, by reason of your holiness, when you stand before God our Father at the coming of our Lord Yeshua with all his angels.

4 Therefore, brothers, just as you learned from us how you had to live to please God, and just as you are living this way now, we ask you—indeed, united with the Lord Yeshua, we urge you—to keep doing so increasingly. For you know what instructions we gave you on the authority of the Lord Yeshua. What God wants is that you be holy, that you keep away from sexual immorality, that each of you know how to manage his sexual impulses in a holy and honorable manner, without giving in to lustful desires, like the pagans who do not know God. No one should wrong his brother in this matter or take advantage of him, because the Lord punishes all who do such things—as we have explained to you before at length. For God did not call us to live an unclean life but a holy one. Therefore, whoever rejects this teaching is rejecting not a man but God, indeed, the One who gives you the *Ruach HaKodesh*, which is his.

Concerning love for the brothers we do not need to write you, for you yourselves have been taught by God to love each other; and you do love all the brothers throughout Macedonia. But we urge you, brothers, to do it even more.

Also, make it your ambition to live quietly, to mind your own business and to earn your living by your own efforts—just as we told you. Then your daily life will gain the respect of outsiders, and you will not be dependent on anyone.

Now, brothers, we want you to know the truth about those who have died; otherwise, you might become sad the way other people do who have nothing to hope for. For since we believe that Yeshua died and rose again, we also believe that in the same way God, through Yeshua, will take with him those who have died. When we say this, we base it on the Lord's own word: we who remain alive when the Lord comes will certainly not take precedence over those who have died. For the Lord himself will come down from heaven with a rousing cry, with a call from one of the ruling angels, and with God's *shofar*; those who died united with the Messiah will be the first to rise; then we who are left still alive will be caught up with them in the clouds to meet the Lord in the air; and thus we will always be with the Lord. So, encourage each other with these words.

5 But you have no need to have anything written to you, brothers, about the times and dates when this will happen; because you yourselves well know that the Day of the Lord will come like a thief in the night. When people are saying, "Everything is so peaceful and secure," then destruction will suddenly come upon them, the way labor pains come upon a pregnant woman, and there is no way they will escape.

But you, brothers, are not in the dark, so that the Day should take you by surprise like a thief; for you are all people who belong to the light, who belong to the day. We do not belong to the night or to darkness, so let us not be asleep, like the rest are; on the contrary, let us stay alert and sober. People who sleep, sleep at night; and people who get drunk, get drunk at night. But since we belong to the day, let us stay sober, **putting on** trust and love **as a breastplate and the hope of being delivered as a helmet**.[1] For God has not intended that we should experience his fury, but that we should gain deliverance through our Lord Yeshua the Messiah, who died on our behalf so that whether we are alive or dead, we may live along with him.

---

1. Isaiah 59:17.

Therefore, encourage each other, and build each other up—just as you are doing.

We ask you, brothers, to respect those who are working hard among you, those who are guiding you in the Lord and confronting you to help you change. Treat them with the highest regard and love because of the work they are doing. Live at peace among yourselves; but we urge you, brothers, to confront those who are lazy, your aim being to help them change, to encourage the timid, to assist the weak, and to be patient with everyone.

See that no one repays evil for evil; on the contrary, always try to do good to each other, indeed, to everyone.

Always be joyful. Pray regularly. In everything give thanks, for this is what God wants from you who are united with the Messiah Yeshua.

Don't quench the Spirit, don't despise inspired messages. But do test everything—hold onto what is good but keep away from every form of evil.

May the God of *shalom* make you completely holy—may your entire spirit, soul and body be kept blameless for the coming of our Lord Yeshua the Messiah. The one calling you is faithful, and he will do it.

Brothers, keep praying for us.

Greet all the brothers with a holy kiss.

I charge you in the Lord to have this letter read to all the brothers.

The grace of our Lord Yeshua the Messiah be with you.

COMMENTARY

Introductory Remarks

First Thessalonians is recognized by scholars as Sha'ul's earliest extant writing. According to Bart Ehrman, "First Thessalonians was, obviously, the first letter Paul wrote to the church in Thessalonica. We do not know how many other letters he wrote to the church there. 1 Thessalonians is Paul's first of an indeterminable number of letters that he wrote to Thessalonica. At least it is the first we know about (not knowing about any others!), but there are reasons from the letter itself for thinking that this is the first letter he wrote to them after leaving their community."[1] This letter was written about 50 C.E.

Sha'ul's first visit to Thessaloniki (Acts 17:1–9) occurred during his second missionary journey, recorded in Acts 15:36–18:22. His initial traveling companion was Sila (Acts 15:40; 17:1; 18:5). During his visit to Derbe, he met Timothy, who accompanied him on his journey (16:1–3; 17:14; 18:5).

---

1 . Bart Ehrman, "What Is Paul's First Surviving Letter All About? 1 Thessalonians." Nov. 25, 2022. https://ehrmanblog.org/what-is-pauls-first-surviving-letter-all-about-1-thessalonians.

FIRST THESSALONIANS
CHAPTER ONE

1:1a. From: Sha'ul,

This letter is unique because unlike most of his other writings, Sha'ul does not identify himself as a *shaliach* (apostle). Sha'ul expresses himself in an intimate and personal manner like a loving and concerned father or brother who is deeply concerned about the members of his family.

1:1b. Sila (Silas/Silvanus),

Sha'ul always refers to Sila as Silvanus (cf. 2 Cor. 1:19; 1 Thess. 1:1; 2 Thess. 1:1), while Luke always calls him Silas. It may be that Silvanus is the Romanized version of the original Silas, or that Silas is the Greek nickname for Silvanus. Catholic theologian Joseph Fitzmyer further points out that *Silas* is the Greek rendition of the Aramaic *Seila* (שְׁאִילָא), a version of the Hebrew *Saul* (שָׁאוּל), attested in Palmyrene inscriptions.[1] His Aramaic and Hebrew name signifies "asked for [from God]." Whether his name indicates he was a Benjaminite as was Sha'ul is speculative. It is interesting to note that Sila was also a Roman citizen (Acts 16:37).[2]

Sila, who is considered to be a prophet (Acts 15:32), was one of the "select men" (Acts 15:22)[3] who was appointed by the Jerusalem Council to accompany Sha'ul to Antioch to inform the Gentiles who

---

1. "Silas." Wikipedia. https://en.wikipedia.org/wiki/Silas#cite_note-Dunn2003-2.
2. Hilary Le Cornu and Joseph Shulam, *A Commentary on the Jewish Roots of Acts*, 842.
3. The other "select men" include Bar-Nabba (Barnabbas), and Y'hudah called Bar-Sabba ((Judas called Barsabbass).

were turning to God of the Council's decision regarding which Torah commandments they were obligated to observe (Acts 15:1–35).[4] Sila and Sha'ul were imprisoned in Philippi, where an earthquake broke their chains and opened the prison door (Acts 16:25–37).

1:1c. And Timothy

Sha'ul first met Timothy in Derbe (Acts 16:1–3). Timothy had a Greek father and Jewish mother. For some reason, though he was Jewish,[5] he was not yet circumcised. As such, the Jewish community would have considered him a gentile foreigner and not a member of the Jewish community, precluding Timothy from participating in Jewish religious activities, limiting his ability to share the Good News with his people.[6] Sha'ul's circumcising Timothy also indicates that Sha'ul was not opposed to Jewish believers maintaining their identity and loyalty to Jewish traditions and customs. In Acts 21:21, Sha'ul is accused of teaching Jewish believers to forsake Moses— specifically mentioning forbidding them to circumcise their children. To invalidate their accusations, Sha'ul undertakes a Nazarite vow (Acts 21:22–26).

Sha'ul considered Timothy his true son in the faith (1 Timothy 1:2), which indicates that Timothy was his talmid (disciple). Most commentators understand "a true son in the faith" to mean Timothy was Sha'ul's convert, though there is nowhere in the Scriptures that explicitly says this. Though Timothy might have been Sha'ul's convert, the phrase "a true son in the faith" indicates a much stronger and more meaningful relationship, namely that of a rabbi and disciple.

---

4. These Torah commandments are known as the Noachide Laws. For a further explanation, see *The Jewish Annotated New Testament*, Note 20, page 239.
5 . Sometime during the first two centuries C.E., Jewish descent became matrilineal, not patrilineal. For an interesting perspective on Timothy's "Jewishness," see Shaye J. D. Cohen, 363–377.
6. Le Cornu and Shulam, *A Commentary*, 861–865.

Timothy's ministry was multifaceted. He was Sha'ul's representative to the Thessalonians, Corinthians, and Philippians (1 Thess. 3:1; (1 Cor. 4:17; Phil. 2:19). He was a pastor and teacher in Ephesus (1 Tim. 1:2–3) and frequently cosigned Sha'ul's letters (e.g., 2 Cor. 1:1; Phil. 1:1; 1 Thess. 1:1; 2 Thess. 1:1; Philem. 1). His name means "honoring God" or "honored by God."

Sha'ul, Sila and Timothy functioned as a team, each one ministering with the various talents and giftings God had given them (Acts 16:4–5;14; 17:1–32).

1:1d. To: The Messianic Community of the Thessalonians,

The word for messianic community often translated "church" or "assembly" is the Greek *ecclesia*, derived from the Hebrew *qahal*. In the Tanakh, Israel is frequently called the assembly of God (Deut. 5:22a; Judg. 20:2; 1 Kgs 8:14).

> Those who heard the term ecclesia in antiquity may have understood a range of meanings, but certainly a political, civic assembly would have been evoked in an urban context (to which Paul's letters are aimed, after all: Meeks 2003). The term in the classical period had referred to the democratic assembly of the city, usually made up of free adult male citizens. At the time of Paul's writings, political assemblies in Greek cities around the Roman Empire still bore the name *ekklēsiai*, or in the singular, *ekklēsia*, and still met to engage in democratic deliberation about what was best for their cities (Miller). Were the *ekklēsiai* to which Paul wrote places of democratic debate and deliberative discourse, of authoritative speeches and challenges to those speeches, of the busy roil of argument, struggle, and the testing of ideas? (Schüssler Fiorenza 1987; 1993)[7]

---

7. Laura Nasrallah, "Chapter-length commentary on 1 Corinthians (Fortress Press)." https://www.academia.edu/7457182.

In the *Brit Chadashah*, the term *ekklēsia/ qahal* has an added dimension. It is related to belief in Yeshua and his imminent return (1 Cor. 7:29; 15:1–58; 1 Thess. 4:13-18). Therefore, the believers at Thessaloniki can be aptly described as the eschatological assembly of God.

Though one of the Hebrew equivalents for synagogue (Greek *synagogue*) is also *qahal,* the Thessalonians eventually met in the home of Jason (Acts 17:6).

1:1e. United with God the Father and the Lord Yeshua the Messiah:

The juxtaposition of the terms "God the Father" with "the Lord Yeshua the Messiah" in Sha'ul's letters is theologically significant (3:11; 1 Cor. 7:17; 8:5–6; 2 Cor. 13:13; 2 Thess. 1:2, 8; 2:16; 3:5). He often assigns them parallel actions (1 Cor. 7:17; 8:5–6; 2 Cor. 13:13; 2 Thess. 2:16; cf. 1 Cor. 12:4–6; 2 Cor. 1:21–22), which points to the concept of Yeshua and the Father being One (John 10:30), which reflects *Logos* theology (John 1:1).

> In the Thessalonian letters the term "Lord" (*Kyrios)* occurs as a designation for Jesus some forty-six times (as calculated by M. Smith 2013, 288; though some examples could refer to God the Father) and has definite divine resonances. In the LXX, the term applied to Yahweh. In Hellenistic politics the term denoted a king, and in Roman religion it designated the emperor; in many contexts it could imply divinity (Suetonius, *Dom.* 13; SEG 12.514; *Mart. Pol.* 8.2; 10.1). The second title used here for Jesus is a translation of the Jewish word messiah, "anointed one." In the OT the term could refer to a prophet (1 Kgs. 19:16), priest (Exod. 29:7), or king (2 Sam. 2:4–7); yet in Second Temple literature it often had divine resonances as well, especially when associated with the "Son of Man" figure (1 En. 52.4; 46.3; 48.2; 62.5; cf. 2 Esd. [4 Ezra]12:32–33; 2 Bar. 40.1–4).[8]

---

8. Timothy A. Brookins, *First and Second Thessalonians*, 58.

1:1f. Grace to you and *shalom*:

A common salutation that appears at least a dozen times in Sha'ul's epistles. Some examples can be found in Romans 1:7; 1 Corinthians 1:3; and 1 Timothy 1:2.

Grace: [*Charis* (Greek) / *chesed* (Hebrew)]. Believers have received an unmerited gift that flows from God's grace (*chesed*). *Chesed* appears 190 times in the Tanakh; its Greek cognate *charis* appears 156 times in the *Brit Chadashah. Chesed* can be understood in a variety of ways. It can be defined as giving oneself fully, with love and compassion. Yeshua's redemption of humanity is the ultimate expression of God's grace, and God's *chesed* is personified as a teacher who instructs a child in the way of righteousness (Titus 2:11). God's *chesed* is the active presence of the *Ruach HaKodesh*, which sustains a believer (2 Cor. 13:14).

Shalom – שָׁלוֹם: Used both as a greeting and farewell, "*shalom*" carries with it the concept of peace, prosperity, harmony, and well-being. The word appears 236 times in the Tanakh, and its Greek cognate *eirēnē* appears 92 times in the Brit Chadashah. For followers of Yeshua, *shalom* is the peace, soundness, health, freedom from worry, and the tranquil state of a soul assured of its salvation that comes through the healing works and forgiving words of Yeshua (Acts 10:36). Yeshua imparts to those who trust in him a *shalom* that surpasses our human understanding.

> Do not worry about anything; on the contrary, make your requests known to God by prayer and petition, with thanksgiving. Then God's shalom, passing all understanding, will keep your hearts and minds safe in union with the Messiah Yeshua. (Phil. 4:6–7; cf. Jn. 14:27, 16:33)

Another cogent example of God's *shalom* is Yosef's response to Pharaoh regarding the interpretation of his troubling dreams. God would answer him with a peaceful explanation and satisfactory solution to avert the coming crisis (Gen. 41:16).

> Yosef answered Pharaoh, "It isn't in me. God will give Pharaoh an answer that will set his mind at peace."

1:3b. how your trust produces action, your love hard work, and your hope perseverance.

Since one of the foundations of the life of a righteous person is hope (Greek *elpis*), it is a prevalent theme in First Thessalonians (1:3, 2:19, 4:13, 5:8). The Greek word for hope[9] is often translated in the *Tanakh* as *betach/bahtach*[10] or *Tikvah*.[11] The two Hebrew words are linked together in Psalm 25:2–3.

> [1] I lift my inner being to you, *ADONAI*;
> [2] I trust (*betach*) you, my God.
> Don't let me be disgraced,
> don't let my enemies gloat over me.
> [3] No one waiting (*tikvah*) for you will be disgraced;
> disgrace awaits those who break faith for no reason.

David Stern expounds upon the scriptural concept of hope:

> And hope is not a vapid wish but the expectation, grounded in God's Word, that he will fulfill his promises to his people (see Rom. 9:1–11:36N); as such, it produces perseverance, patience, endurance (compare Rom. 5:2–5,8:20–25; MJ 6:11).

> But for now, three things last—trust, *hope*, love; and the greatest of these is love" (1 Cor. 13:13). Here, however, Sha'ul mentions *hope* at the end of the list to emphasize it, because a major problem in the Thessalonian Messianic community was

---

9. Also translated as confidence, trust, hope, or to wait.
10. Psalm 25:2; Isaiah 12:2.
11. Psalm 25:3; Proverbs 20:2.

misunderstanding the nature of our hope in the Messiah's Second Coming, with impatience and laziness among the consequences (v. 10; 2:19; 3:13; 4:13–5:6; 2 Thess. 1:7–10; 2:1–12; 3:6–15).[12]

1:5. The Good News we brought did not become for you a matter only of words, but also one of power, the *Ruach HaKodesh* and total conviction—just as you know how we lived for your sakes when we were with you.

Previous to Shavuot (Acts 2), the active presence of the power of the *Ruach HaKodesh* (the Holy Spirit), which sustains each believer (2 Cor. 13:14), was limited to specific individuals such as Moses and the elders of Israel (Num. 11:17–25), Othniel and Gideon, who were among the Judges of Israel (Judg. 3:10, 6:34), and King David (Ps. 51:11).The *Ruach*, also called the Counselor, reveals God's thoughts, which enables one to understand the mind of God (Jn. 14:26). The Holy Spirit leads and guides each believer into all truth (Jn. 16:13) including the truth regarding the details of the coming of the Lord (1 Thess. 1:10, 4:13–18).

1:6–8a. You, indeed, became imitators of us and of the Lord; so that even though you were going through severe troubles, you received the Word with joy from the *Ruach HaKodesh*.[7] Thus you became a pattern for all the believers in Macedonia and Achaia; [8] for the Lord's message sounded forth from you not only in Macedonia and Achaia, but everywhere your trust toward God became known.

With loving encouragement, Sha'ul reminds the Thessalonians that the *Ruach* also empowers believers to withstand persecution such as Steven (Acts 6:5–7:59) in the power of his might (Eph. 6:10–18).

---

12. David H. Stern, *Jewish New Testament Commentary: A Companion Volume to the Jewish New Testament*, 616.

The concept of imitating Sha'ul's godly behavior is another prevalent theme in his writings (1 Cor. 4:14–17, 11:1; Eph. 5:1; Phil. 4:9). Sha'ul reminds the Thessalonians that "as a father treats his children, we encouraged you and comforted you and appealed to you to lead lives worthy of God, who calls you into his Kingdom and glory" (1 Thess. 2:11–12).

In Judaism, teachers are frequently portrayed as father figures (*B. Sanhedrin* 19b); thus, when Sha'ul addresses the Thessalonians as his "children" he is, by common practice, identifying them as his *talmidim*. Reinhard Neudecker states: "The rabbinic interpretation of biblical 'father' and 'son' as 'master' and 'disciple' is common,"[13] and, according to Daniel Boyarin, "becoming a 'disciple of the Sages' often meant accepting a rabbinic father in place of one's biological father." [14] The Book of Knowledge https://www.chabad.org/library/article_cdo/aid/910970/jewish/Talmud-Torah.htm*Talmud Torah* (*Sefer Mada*), also called The Laws of Torah Study, exemplifies the idea that becoming a "disciple of the Sages" often meant not only accepting a rabbinic father in place of one's biological father but that the role of a rabbi could even supersede that of a father.

> There is no greater honor than that due a teacher, and no greater awe than that due a teacher. Our Sages declared: "Your fear of your teacher should be equivalent to your fear of Heaven."[15]

---

13. Reinhard Neudecker, "Master-disciple/disciple-master relationship in rabbinic Judaism and in the gospels," *Gregorianum* vol. 80, no. 2 (1999), 245–261.
14. Daniel Boyarin, *The Talmud: A Personal Take – Selected Essays*. See the story of Rabbi Eliezer ben Hyrcanus in Judah Goldin, *The Fathers According to Rabbi Nathan, 43* (chap. 6), and parallels.
15. *Sefer Mada*.

Samuel Lachs connects these statements in Talmud Torah 5:1 with Luke 14:26, which, in a similar fashion, declares that a *talmid's* rabbi is to be more highly esteemed than one's father.[16]

> If anyone comes to me and does not hate his father, his mother, his wife, his children, his brothers, and his sisters, yes, and his own life besides, he cannot be my *talmid* (Lk. 14:26).

1:10. Wait for his Son Yeshua, whom he raised from the dead, to appear from heaven and rescue us from the impending fury of God's judgment.

The appearance of the Messiah at the End of Days permeates the Scriptures. While traditional Jews are waiting for the Messiah's one and only appearance, Messianic believers such as the Thessalonians were and still are anticipating Yeshua's return, often called the second coming.

Balaam's prophecy concerning "the star that shall come out of Jacob and the scepter that shall rise out of Israel" (Num. 24:17) has been interpreted by Jewish exegetes as referring to the coming of King Mashiach to redeem Israel from her enemies. Maimonides clearly understands 24:17-18 as referring to the Messianic King. However, the arrival of the King is relegated to an unspecified time in the future.[17] Whoever does not believe in him, or does not await his coming, denies not only [the statements of] the other prophets, but also [those of] the Torah and of Moshe, our teacher, for the Torah attests to his coming, stating in Deuteronomy 30:3–5...[18]

---

16. Samuel Tobias Lachs, *A Rabbinic Commentary on The New Testament: The Gospels of Matthew, Mark and Luke*, 187.
17. Moses Maimonides and Eliyahu Touger, *Mishneh Torah*.
18. Yad Hil. Melakim 9.1

> At that point, *ADONAI* your God will reverse your exile and show you mercy; he will return and gather you from all the peoples to which *ADONAI* your God scattered you. If one of yours was scattered to the far end of the sky, *ADONAI* your God will gather you even from there; he will go there and get you. *ADONAI* your God will bring you back into the land your ancestors possessed, and you will possess it; he will make you prosper there, and you will become even more numerous than your ancestors.

Much of the speculation as to the timing of the last days was also based on the exegeses of Daniel 7:25, which Silver calls "the *locus classicus* of messianic prophecy." Balaam and Daniel both speak about the events that will take place at the end of time. While Balaam gives no specific date for the last days, Daniel does. Thus, by knowing the specific time when Daniel's prophecy would be fulfilled, one could know when Balaam's Fourth prophecy would be fulfilled.[19]

The Scriptures in the Synoptic Gospels that describe the return of Yeshua have been designated by scholars as "The Synoptic Apocalypse," a modern scholarly designation for the apocalyptic material and a reworking of Second Temple Jewish apocalyptic eschatology best preserved in Matthew.

> Some of the Scriptures that are included in the Synoptic Apocalypse are Matt. 24:30; Mark 13:26; and Luke 21:27 (Flusser 301). Each verse includes the term "Son of Man," which is an allusion to Daniel 7:13 (Gaebelein 505). The accepted theory is that these verses are rooted in the literature of Apocalyptic Judaism (Albright; Mann 288). Rudolf Bultmann concurs. The phrase "Son of Man" is a Greek translation of the

---

19. Abba Hillel Silver, *Messianic Speculation in Israel*, 3.

Aramaic *bar enosh* which is attested to in several pre-Christian Syrian and Palestinian texts (Sefire III 16; 1Qap-Gen 21:13; 11QtgJob 9:9; 26:3) (Fitzmier 208).[20]

The Synoptic Apocalypse is classified as "eschatological prophecy," because it predicts the coming of the Son of Man, and its proclamation is consistent with the method and the message of Jewish Apocalyptic literature (Russell 340–350). Whether Yeshua was aware of additional works of Jewish apocalyptic literature such as *First Enoch* (300–200 B.C.E.) and *The Similitudes of Enoch* (2nd century B.C.E.) is unknown. Daniel Boyarin in *The Jewish Gospels* maintains that Yeshua understood himself to embody of the career of "the one like a Son of Man" as seen in the Book of Daniel.

Keil and Delitzsch affirm Boyarin's contention. If then Yeshua speaks of himself as the Son of Man, he means not merely that he was the Messiah, but he wishes to designate himself as the Messiah of Daniel's prophecy.[21]

Daniel 7:13–14 reads:

"I kept watching the night visions,
when I saw, coming with the clouds of heaven,
someone like a son of man.
He approached the Ancient One
and was led into his presence.
To him was given rulership,
glory and a kingdom,
so that all peoples, nations and languages

---

20. Yosef Koelner, *Cosmic Warfare: The Final Destruction of Amalek by the Messianic King*, 53–56.
21. Koelner, *Cosmic Warfare*, 53–56.

should serve him.
His rulership is an eternal rulership
that will not pass away;
and his kingdom is one
that will never be destroyed.

In 1 Thessalonians 4:13-18, Sha'ul expounds upon the resurrection of the dead (*Techiyat HaMetim*), which is another one of the components of the Synoptic Apocalypse.

FIRST THESSALONIANS
CHAPTER TWO

2:1. You yourselves know, brothers, that our visit to you was not fruitless.

Sha'ul recounts his ministry at Thessaloniki. He expresses his affection for the Thessalonians with Kinship Metaphors, [1] as members of his family utilizing terms such as "brothers," which includes both males and females who are members of God's family (cf. 2:1,9, 14, 17; 3:7; 4:1, 12, 14, 25, 27) as well as the more authoritative parental metaphors of a mother nursing and caring for her children (2:7; cf. Isa. 66:13), and as a father who encourages and comforts his children (2:11).

2:2. On the contrary, although we had already suffered and been outraged in Philippi, as you know, we had the courage, united with our God, to tell you the Good News even under intense pressure.

He comforts and encourages his children by self-identifying with their suffering (2:2; cf. Phil. 1:29–30). Rabbi Jonathan Sacks explains that empathy is powerful because empathy sees the world through someone else's eyes, enters into their feelings and acts in such a way as to let them know that they are understood, that they are heard and that they matter. [2] Empathy, a fundamental principal of Judaism, appears in the Torah thirty-six times—a prime example being *Shemot* (Exod. 23:9).

---

1. Trevor J. Burke, *Family Matters: A Socio-Historical Study of Kinship Metaphors in 1 Thessalonians*.
2. https://www.rabbisacks.org/covenant-conversation/mishpatim/the-power-of-empathy/#_ftn2.

"You shall not oppress a stranger, for you know the soul [the feelings, thoughts, and concerns] of a stranger, for you were strangers in Egypt."

2:3. For the appeal we make does not flow from error or from impure motives, neither do we try to trick people.

Throughout his ministry Sha'ul is constantly accused of misconduct (Acts 21:21, 27–29; 1 Cor. 9:1–27; Gal. 1:10). As a result, he frequently finds it necessary to defend himself (Acts 22:1–30, 24:10–27; 1 Cor. 11:16–17, 21, 23; 12:6, 11). At Thessaloniki he is accused of proclaiming a false Messiah to Jews and Gentiles (Acts 17:1–9; 1 Thess. 2:15).

2:7. As emissaries of the Messiah, we could have made our weight felt; but instead, we were gentle when we were with you, like a mother feeding and caring for her children.

In his salutation Sha'ul does not refer to himself as an emissary (*shaliach*), but in the light of the criticism he has received, and in defense of his ministry's legitimacy, he reaffirms himself and his companions as a divinely appointed apostles who have been sent to Thessaloniki by the Messiah Yeshua.

Hermann Vogelstein clearly states that the concept of the *shaliach* "must be understood from a historical point of view as having developed out of the Jewish apostolate."[3] In its Jewish context, *shaliach* can be a person "who, whether a man or woman, was the agent or emissary of the sender: the concept of *shaliah shel' adam kemoto* ['a person's agent is as the person himself'] and thus fully representative of the sender."[4] Inherent in this definition is the idea of being chosen as a representative of a higher power such as

---

3. Hermann Volgelstein, "The Development of the Apostolate in Judaism and Its Transformation in Christianity," https://www.jstor.org/stable/23502509.
4. Levine and Brettler, *Jewish Annotated New Testament*, 112.

God or a king and of having the authority to transmit the message of the one who sent him. Vogelstein says, "This office was found as early as the time of the composition of the Books of Chronicles. Two categories of apostles [*shaliach*] could be ascertained, viz. (1) apostles of the central authorities to the various communities, and (2) apostles of the communities to the various central authorities."[5]

Ezra is an example of the prototype *shaliach* as he was sent as the representative (*shaliach*) of King Artaxerxes to the Jewish community in Jerusalem (Ezra 7:14). In a similar fashion, Artaxerxes sends Nehemiah to Jerusalem to authorize the rebuilding of the city of Jerusalem (Neh. 2:5).

In the *Brit Chadashah* (New Covenant), one of the clearest examples of the Jewish concept of an apostle can be found in the Synoptic Gospels where Yeshua appoints or commissions his twelve *talmidim* (disciples) as *shlikhim* (apostles) (Mt. 10:1–2; cf. Mk. 3:13–19a; Lk. 6:12–16). According to Heinrich Schuetz, the phrase "sent out" as it appears in Mark is the literal translation of a Hebrew expression that in all cases means "to appoint as a plenipotentiary (an authorized representative)."

As Sha'ul had been commissioned by Yeshua (Acts 9:3–6) and his calling had been affirmed by the Apostles in Jerusalem (9:26–28), the Messianic community in Thessaloniki, whose core constituency was comprised of Jewish people and God-fearers, would have been familiar with the office of a *shaliach* and should have enabled them to accept the full weight of Sha'ul's authority and message. As a Pharisee, Sha'ul was quite familiar with the ministry of a *shaliach*. Matthew 23:15 demonstrates (confirms) the Pharisees embraced the concept of being sent to a particular community as a *shaliach*.

---

5. Yosef Koelner and Jeffrey Seif, *Sha'ul / Paul God's Shaliach (Apostle) Corresponds With The 1 Corinthians – Restoring a Congregation in Crisis – 2 Corinthians – Countering Messianic Madness*, 26–27.

"Woe to you hypocritical Torah-teachers and *P'rushim*! You go about [as a *shaliach*] over land and sea to make one proselyte; and when you succeed, you make him twice as fit for Gei-Hinnom as you are!" (Mt. 23:15)

His own criticism of those who misused the role only serves to emphasize his care to uphold the integrity of his own calling.

2:10. You are witnesses, and so is God, of how holy, righteous and blameless our behavior was in the sight of you believers;

According to E. P. Sanders, terms such as "blameless" are in accord with the principles of righteous behavior as found in the Torah and Jewish Tradition.[6] As a Pharisee, Sha'ul would have a favorable (positive) concern for both moral and ritual purity. [7] Sanders explains: "The same was true of a lot of Jews and of a lot of pagans. Even Paul was concerned with his own brand of purity. Such words as 'purity' (*hagneia*), 'holy' or 'sanctified' (*hagios*), 'without blemish' (*amomos*), 'cleanse' or 'purify' (*katharizo*), along with many others, were widely used in the ancient world and used in a favorable way."

"Blameless" is also a legal term indicating a person who is above reproach who cannot be charged with an accusation. (cf. 1 Cor 1: 8; Col. 1:22; 1 Tim 3:10). Believers who are judged blameless at the time of the *parousia* will inherit the Kingdom of God (1 Cor. 6:9–10; Gal 5:19–21; Eph. 5:5).[8]

2:14–16. For, brothers, you came to be imitators of God's congregations in Y'hudah that are united with the Messiah Yeshua—you suffered the same things from your countrymen as they did from

---

6. E. P. Sanders, *Paul, the Law, and the Jewish People*, 23, 94.
7. Jacob Neusner, *Judaism in the Beginning of Christianity*, 57–59.
8. Karl P. Donfried & I. Howard Marshall, eds., *The Theology of the Shorter Pauline Letters*.

the Judeans who both killed the Lord Yeshua and the prophets and chased us out too. They are displeasing God and opposing all mankind by trying to keep us from speaking to the Gentiles, so that they may be delivered. Their object seems to be always to make their sins as bad as possible! But God's fury will catch up with them in the end.

One of the most difficult and controversial sections of Scripture is found in these verses because their misinterpretation forms the basis of classical Christian antisemitism.[9]

Michael Rydelnik, who is not a proponent of the traditional interpretation of 1 Thessalonians 2:14–16, summarizes this misinterpretation:

> These verses contain a blanket condemnation of the Jews as a nation. They are not in contradiction with Romans 9–11 because they reflect a cry of anguish (without any hope) as well as a shout of anger. They teach that the Jews as a nation are chiefly responsible for the death of Jesus, and for this reason Paul was not contradicting Acts 4:27–28 and the historical record. This view holds that Paul was condemning the guiltiest group.[10]

Note that I have included in the Addenda Michael Rydelnik's complete article *Was Paul Anti-Semitic? Revisiting 1 Thessalonians 2:14–16*, an in-depth explanation of these misinterpreted verses.

I agree with Rabbi Michael J. Cook's thesis that these antisemitic interpretations are rooted in the development of "historical antisemitism," which commenced with the Jewish revolt and other exigencies in the 60s A.D. and intensified with the Church Fathers and beyond, for the purpose of creating Christian traditions to

---

9. Amy-Jill Levine, *Jewish Annotated New Testament*, 374.
10. Michael A. Rydelnik, "Was Paul Anti-Semitic? Revisiting 1 Thessalonians 2:14–16." *Galaxie* Winter 2023. https://www.galaxie.com/article/bsac165-657-06.

punctuate their retellings about Yeshua with literary devices that shifted responsibility (expressed as "blame") for his death from Rome onto the entire Jewish nation. According to Cook, this development, later intensified especially by Rome's fourth-century adoption of Christianity, congealed into aspersion of the Jews as the "Christ Killers."[11]

The principal historical obstacles which prevent one from correctly interpreting the text are contextual, morphological, grammatical, and textual interpolations.

Contextual

The proper exegesis of verses 2:14–16 is context-dependent. One needs to understand how the Thessalonians and first-century secular readers would have understood Sha'ul's letter to the Thessalonians. Unfortunately, theology has eclipsed the historical context.

Annette Yoshiko Reed reports that recent literary studies of the New Testament have suggested that many of these statements referring to Jews only refer to specific groups of Jews at the time, and hold different meanings when read in context, and/or make sense when framed as inner-Jewish debates.[12] Markus Bockmuehl concurs:

> It is of course true that both the Dead Sea sectarians and even a writer like Josephus can accuse Jerusalemites of exhibiting qualities reminiscent of those alleged by Paul. In their sweeping generality, however, there can be little doubt that Paul's assertions here are particularly marked by an element of passionate Middle Eastern hyperbole, as it moves from the aorist

11. Michael J. Cook, *Modern Jews Engage the New Testament: Enhancing Jewish Well-Being in a Christian Environment*, 130.
12. Paula Fredriksen and Adele Reinhartz, *Jesus, Judaism and Christian Anti-Judaism: Reading the New Testament After the Holocaust*, 8.

tense to the present, from specific allegations into the realm of caricature, and thus from the particular to the categorical. Daniel Marguerat has rightly documented the "rhetoric of excess" that permeates chapter 2 and the continuation of such rhetoric in 2:14–16 confirms the impression of a consistent rhetorical *Sitz im Le ben.*[13]

Context determines the appropriate translation of the word "Jew(s)" due to its various shades of meaning.

Morphological

Morphological because the definition of the Greek word for "Jew(s)" (*Ioudaíos/Iioudaias*), when translated into multiple languages, is not understood in context-dependent ways. Instead, it is simply translated as "the Jews," which implies the homogeneous group of people who killed Yeshua.

The following definitions of the word "Jew" have been collated from the *Theological Dictionary of the New Testament*, pp. 356–391, which includes its usage in Hellenistic Judaism including Philo and Josephus, Greek Hellenistic literature such as Plutarch, and in the New Testament.

All three groups, depending on the context, normally use "Jews" to designate a nation (often within the context of its language, script, measures, coins or names of the months), a specific region that was allotted to the tribe of Judah, an ethnic group regardless of religious practice, both ethnic Jews and proselytes who practice the religion of Judaism, and in a restrictive sense that specifies Jewish individuals or groups.

---

13. Markus Bockmuehl, "1 Thessalonians 2:14–16 and the Church in Jerusalem." *Tyndale Bulletin*, May 1, 2001. https://doi.org/10.53751/001c.30258.

The word-group for "Jew(s)" appears most frequently in the Book of John and, with rare exceptions, is reflective of its use in the New Testament.

> Among the many uses in John, we note first a similarity to that of the Synoptics in the passion story (18:33, 39; 19:3), where "king of the Jews" occurs on non-Jewish lips (cf. also 18:35). It is also a Samaritan woman who speaks in 4:5, and distinction is made from the Samaritans in 4:22. (ii) John also uses Ιουδαία for inhabitants of Palestine, especially in explanation of Jewish customs or circumstances. The aim is obviously to make things clear to foreigners (cf. 2:6, 13; 5:1; 7:2). In such contexts the use is objective and nonemphatic. The same applies to 1:19; 3:1, etc. Some of these Jews may well be believers in Jesus (8:31; 11:45; 12:11). This usage corresponds to that of Josephus and need not imply that the author himself is distant in time or nationality. (iii) In some passages the Jews in John are opponents of Jesus, though opposition arises from the context and is not implicit in the term. Thus, certain Jews criticize Jesus as such because he rejects the temple in 2:18ff. or calls himself the bread of life in 6:41ff. or claims unity with the Father in 10:31 (cf. also 5:16ff.; 8:48; 13:33). Some Jews take up an ambiguous attitude for fear of the Jews (7:13; 9:22). The point in all this is not that the Jews as a whole reject Jesus, or that a specific group of Zealots does so, but that opposition arises on the grounds of the Jewish religion (cf. 9:29). A gulf is thus implied between the Christian understanding of the OT and the Jewish understanding which resists it. For John, the Jews are often those who adopt this Jewish understanding in rejection of Jesus. At the same time, the national basis remains. Not all Jews reject Jesus, and those who do so are first Jews by nationality, and only then Jews in opposition to Jesus.[14]

---

14 . Gerhard Kittel, Gerhard Friedrich, and G. W. Bromiley, *Theological Dictionary of the New Testament*, 332.

Grammatical

It is common knowledge that ancient texts were almost always written without punctuation. Any commas, periods, question marks and the like are later additions by editors and translators that have been inserted in some later manuscripts of First Thessalonians. Such additions alter the intended meaning of the text as evidenced in a myriad of translations including the Greek, German, and English versions.

Dr. Yeshaya Gruber poses the following question: Can punctuation be anti-Jewish? He answers his own question with this statement:

> At least one scholar thinks so. Frank Gilliard has argued that a single comma gave generations of Christians a very wrong impression of the Jewish people, tragically leading to much antisemitism throughout history. In 1 Thessalonians 2:14–15, most English translations have something like "…the Jews, who both killed the Lord Jesus and the prophets, and drove us out" (NASB). That sounds like an extremely strong anti-Jewish statement. *But what if there should be no comma after the word "Jews"?*[15]

The following is Frank D. Gilliard's thesis regarding the insertion of a comma:

> How could Paul, a proud Jew and Pharisee, so categorically condemn his own people? And how can so early and sweeping a condemnation be explained by scholars who argue that such virulent antisemitism did not in fact develop until the latter part of the century, after the destruction of the Temple and the council at Jamnia?

---

15. Dr. Yeshaya Gruber, "Can a Comma Be Antisemitic?" *Israel Bible Center*, July 27, 2023, https://weekly.israelbiblecenter.com/can-a-comma-be-antisemitic.

… the comma that separates verse 14 from verse 15 in both the modern Greek text and in most translations of the passage, allowing (in the RSV) [to read]: 'for you suffered the same things from your countrymen as they did from the Jews, (15) who killed both the Lord Jesus and the prophets, and drove us out…'

Such a comma is used in English to set off nonrestrictive (or non-limiting) relative clauses. In this sentence it signifies that 'the Jews' in effect means 'all Jews,' and that the relative clause that follows does not restrict that inclusive meaning. With the comma, the 'denunciation is unqualified, no hope for the future is expressed.' If there were no comma, Paul would be inveighing against specifically restricted groups of Jews.[16]

Thus, the choice of punctuation can make an enormous difference for the meaning of a sentence. Similarly, if someone writes, "We must oppose the judges who take bribes," this sounds like a good and principled stand in favor of justice and against a minority of corrupt judges. However, if someone else writes, "We must oppose the judges, who take bribes," the use of the comma implies that *all* the judges are corrupt and must be resisted. (In grammatical terms, this is the difference between a restrictive and a nonrestrictive clause.)[17]

Interpolations

Interpolations because authors such as F. C. Baur conclude that this passage "has a thoroughly un-Pauline stamp and that the reproach against the Jews reflects a later period, at a time when Pauline Christianity was seeking an accommodation with Jewish Christianity, and the Jews were regarded on all sides as enemies of the gospel."

16. Frank D. Gilliard, "The Problem of the Antisemitic Comma between 1 Thessalonians 2.14 and 15." *New Testament Studies*, Cambridge University Press, February 5, 2009. https://doi.org/10.1017/S0028688500015162, 481–482.
17. Gruber, "Can a Comma Be Antisemitic?"

Baur saw in this passage a powerful argument against the authenticity of 1 Thessalonians as a whole; this solution is, of course, unsatisfactory. Some (though certainly not all) 19th-century scholars suggested the difficulties could be solved by the hypothesis of later interpolation. Albrecht Ritschl proposed to excise 1 Thessalonians 2:16c as a scribal gloss post-70 referring to the destruction of Jerusalem. He was followed subsequently by several other scholars such as Schmiedel and Holtzmann.[18] Rabbi Cook also maintains that 1 Thessalonians 2:14–16 is a post-70 interpolation where theology eclipses history.[19]

However, it is highly unlikely that 1 Thessalonians is an interpolation because the textual evidence of for the interpolation of 1 Thessalonians 2:13–16 is nonexistent. While the issue of interpolation cannot be dismissed out of hand, there is no compelling exegetical or historical reason to consider 1 Thess. 2:13-16, or any part of it, a post-Pauline interpolation.

Most modern scholars argue against interpolation, including Markus Bockmuehl, "1 Thessalonians 2:14–16 and the Church in Jerusalem"; Gene L. Green, *The Letters to the Thessalonians*; Jeffrey S. Lamp, "Is Paul Anti-Jewish? Testament of Levi 6 in the Interpretation of 1 Thessalonians 2:13–16"; and Abraham Malherbe, *The Letters to the Thessalonians*.[20]

---

18 . Birger A. Pearson, "1 Thessalonians 2:13–16: A Deutero-Pauline Interpolation." *The Harvard Theological Review* 64.1 (1971), 79–94. https://www.jstor.org/stable/1508972.

19. Cook, *Modern Jews Engage the New Testament*, 130.

20. Brenton Dickieson, "Antisemitism and the Judaistic Paul: A Study of I Thessalonians 2:14–16 in Light of Paul's Social and Rhetorical Contexts and the Contemporary Question of Antisemitism." Dissertation. https://www.academia.edu/4033038.

Interpreting the Text Within Its Original Context

In these verses, Sha'ul is simply stating there are similarities between the opposition Thessalonian believers received from their countrymen, some who may have been Jews born in Thessaloniki (Acts 17:5–9) was similar in nature to the opposition that the Jewish believers in Judea received from their fellow countrymen.

These verses are not meant to be understood as saying that the Jewish people as a nation are responsible for the death of Yeshua. To reiterate, in a similar context, John uses the term "the Jews" (Judaeans) to refer to those Jewish leaders who opposed Yeshua and were responsible along with the Romans for his crucifixion (John 1:19,24; 7:13; 9:22; 10:19–21; 18:14).

2:16b. But God's fury will catch up with them in the end.

Many commentators have tried to determine which historical or eschatological event Sha'ul was alluding to, but there is still no scholarly consensus, only conjecture. Based on 5:4, God's fury is associated with the Day of the Lord,[21] which will occur at the end of days (*Acharit Hayamim*). The phrase *Acharit Hayamim* appears in Numbers 24:14, which is followed by the description of the final defeat of Amalek by the Messianic King and the establishment of the Kingdom of God where he will reign forever and ever (Num. 24:15–25; cf. Dan. 7:9-14).

2:17–18. Brothers … deprived … as orphans… We wanted so much to come to you—I, Sha'ul, tried more than once—but the Adversary stopped us.

Sha'ul continues to utilize kinship metaphors to convey his deep connection as well as his love and affection for the Thessalonians.

---

21. Please refer to my comments on chapter 5.

"Deprived" is an expression that indicates a parent's loss of a child.[22] The word "orphan" expresses his profound anguish and describes a person who has, through death, been permanently separated from his parents. He says the Adversary, Satan, has prevented him from coming to see his beloved Thessalonian family.

Sha'ul does not specify the nature of Satan's hindrance. Robert L. Thomas suggests it might have been an illness (cf. 2 Cor. 12:7).[23] Amy-Jill Levine and Marc Zvi Brettler point out that Sha'ul mentions Satan often in connection with his time in Corinth (e.g., 1 Cor. 5.5; 7.5.10.10; 2 Cor. 2.11; 4.4; 6.15; 12.7). In 1 Thessalonians 3:5 he again refers to Satan, calling him the "tempter," a role he plays in rabbinic literature as well; however, neither Paul nor the rabbis portray Satan as the embodiment of evil. Sha'ul interpreted him in terms of the eschatological struggle between good and evil (cf. 1 Thess. 5:5). He does not refer to a physical encounter with Satan but rather a struggle that is characteristic of a world during the period immediately before the new age begins.[24]

The simplest solution is to understand the nature of the obstacle to his coming in a metaphorical sense:

> Jason and the other leaders of the Messianic community had agreed to bind themselves to a security pledge [i.e., bond] (*hikanon*) that guaranteed that Sha'ul and Silas would leave the city and not return (Acts 17:9).[25] In other words, the law of the land had become a tool of the Adversary.

2:19. For when our Lord Yeshua returns,

---

22. J. B. Lightfoot and E. Selwyn Hughes, *Notes on Epistles of St Paul from Unpublished Commentaries*, 45.

23 . Frank E. Gaebelein, *The Expositor's Bible Commentary: Volume 11: Ephesians Through Philemon*, 263.

24. Levine, *Jewish Annotated New Testament*, 374–375.

25. Arnold G. Fruchtenbaum, *Ariel's Bible Commentary: The Book of Acts*, 362.

Though Satan may have blocked Sha'ul and his companions from returning to Thessaloniki, he cannot prevent Yeshua's return to gather up his people. This is the first passage in 1 Thessalonians that introduces the Greek word *parousia* (cf. 1 Thess. 3:13; 4:15; 5:23). In the Greek-speaking world, *parousia* was a technical term that referred to the arrival of Caesar, a governor or other important person on an official state visit. Such a coming always entailed preparation for that person's reception, and it often marked (for dating purposes) the beginning of a new era.[26] Yeshua's return was analogous to a visit from Caesar.

Sha'ul's opponents in Thessaloniki had understood his analogy when they proclaimed:

> "These men who have turned the whole world upside down have come here too! And Jason has let them stay in his home! All of them are defying the decrees of the Emperor (Caesar); because they assert that there is another king, Yeshua!" (Acts 17:6–7)

---

26. David J. Williams, *Paul's Metaphors: Their Context and Character*, 201.

First Thessalonians
Chapter Three

3:1–2. So, when we could no longer stand it, we agreed to be left in Athens alone and sent Timothy, our brother and God's fellow worker for the Good News of the Messiah, to make you solid and encourage you in your trust;

Sha'ul, writing from Corinth, reiterates his concerns, support, and love for the Thessalonians. He sends Timothy, who was not included in the edict that prevented Sha'ul and Silas from returning to Thessaloniki (Acts 17:6–9), to encourage and strengthen the believers during a time of persecution.

3:3–5. so that none of you would let these persecutions unsettle him. For you yourselves know that these are bound to come to us; even when we were with you, we kept telling you in advance that we were about to be persecuted; and indeed, it has happened, as you know. That is the reason, after I could stand it no longer, I sent to find out about your trust. I was afraid that somehow the Tempter had tempted you, and our hard work had been wasted.

The persecution Sha'ul may have been referring to was that of the false prophets and teachers who were opposed to his message (2 Thess. 2:1–2). It seems likely these false prophets and teachers were members of the Circumcision Faction (Acts 15:5, 21:20; Gal. 2:12; Titus 1:10) who Sha'ul sarcastically labels "super apostles," sent by the Tempter to be a "thorn in his flesh" (2 Cor. 12:1–11; cf. 3:5).

David Stern explains: "The 'Circumcision Faction' refers to a subgroup of Messianic Jews, namely, those who insisted that Gentiles could not join the Messianic Community merely by trusting in God and his Messiah Yeshua; they had to become Jewish proselytes. This faction would have consisted of saved Jews who, in their former life as non-Messianic Jews, considered 'God-fearers' (10:2), fence-straddlers that ought to convert to Judaism. Faith in Yeshua would not have made them change their opinion, because the possibility that Gentiles could be members of the Messianic Community without becoming Jews had never arisen."[1]

Sha'ul responds to the false prophets: "Even when we were with you, we kept telling you in advance that we were about to be persecuted; and indeed, it has happened, as you know."

David E. Aune categorizes this verse as a prophetic utterance concerning persecution, originally delivered orally and now in the process of being fulfilled (cf. Acts 20:23).[2]

Sha'ul was concerned the Thessalonians might not be able to pass the test (persecution) that had been set before them by the Tempter. The Greek word for Tempter means "to test" or "to be put to proof."

3:6–8. But now Timothy has come to us from you, bringing good news about your trust and love, and telling us that you remember us well and are always longing to see us, just as we long to see you. Because of this, brothers, despite all our trouble and distress, we were comforted over you—because of your trust; so that now we are alive; since you continue to stand fast, united with the Lord.

Sha'ul thanks God for the "good news" that the Thessalonians were passing the test. Despite severe persecution, they were maintaining their faith. Though he is their "spiritual father," in chapter 3 he uses his favorite and most frequently used familial

---

1. Stern, *Jewish New Testament Commentary*, 619.
2. David Edward Aune, *Prophecy in Early Christianity and the Ancient Mediterranean World*, 259.

expression "brother(s)"—which he employs in this letter no less than 19 times. (1.4; 2.1, 9, 14, 17, etc.).[3]

3:9–11. Indeed, how can we thank God enough for you or express to our God all the joy we feel because of you? Night and day we pray as hard as we can that we will be able to see you face to face and supply whatever shortcomings there may be in your trust. May God our Father and our Lord Yeshua direct our way to you.

The reference to praying night and day (3:10, 5:17) is to the evening (*Ma'ariv*) and morning (*Shacharit*) prayers that regularly take place in the synagogue. These verses imply that the Thessalonian believers had incorporated Jewish liturgy as an integral component of their service structure.

3:13. So that he may give you the inner strength to be blameless, by reason of your holiness, when you stand before God our Father at the coming of our Lord Yeshua with all his angels.

Secular authorities of the Roman colony of Corinth "recorded on inscriptions that Julius Caesar was its founding father and recognized the jurisdiction of the present emperor by attributing the same title to him."[4] Here Sha'ul was saying that though the secular authorities may consider Caesar their father, their true father is God, and in the future, it is not Caesar who will come and bring permanent peace to their city, but rather, on the Day of the Lord, it is Yeshua who will come to establish God's Kingdom (5:1–3).

---

3. Burke, *Family Matters*, 4.
4. Williams, *Paul's Metaphors*, 74.

FIRST THESSALONIANS
CHAPTER FOUR

4:1. Therefore, brothers, just as you learned from us how you had to live to please God,

In 2:10 Sha'ul already stated, "You are witnesses, and so is God, of how holy, righteous and blameless our behavior was in the sight of you believers." He and his companions are models of blameless behavior that pleases God which subsequently prepares a person to participate in the *parousia*.

4:2. For you know what instructions we gave you on the authority of the Lord Yeshua.

The word "instructions" can be defined as an authoritative announcement in the form of a commandment that has directly been given by Yeshua to his disciples (Mt. 10:5; Mk. 6:8; Acts 1:4, 10:42; 1 Cor. 7:10). Therefore, Sha'ul's instructions are

> the authoritative "halakhic" will of God for converted Gentiles, which is the "law [Torah] of the Christ." This might be seen as consisting of the "words of the Lord" as filled out by a body of Torah-based ethical teaching related in some way to the notion of Noachide commandments (Acts 15:19–21) which is common in Jewish tradition applied to all the nations).[1]

Sha'ul frequently alludes to the sayings of Yeshua. In his classic book *Paul and Rabbinic Judaism*, W. D. Davies states:

---

1. Markus Bockmuehl, *Revelation and Mystery in Ancient Judaism and Pauline Christianity*, 155.

We gather that in addition to any traditional material that Sha'ul used he had also the words of Yeshua to which he turned for guidance and makes it clear that when there is an explicit word uttered by Christ on any question, that word is accepted by him as authoritative. Moreover, at the most personal point of all his Epistles we cannot help tracing the impact of the teaching of Yeshua.[2]

Some of the sayings attributed to Yeshua, such as "It is more blessed to give than receive" (Acts 20:35), do not appear in the Gospels and may have been included in a yet-undiscovered collection of the sayings of Yeshua such as the hypothetical Q document. Such a collection is alluded to in Luke 1:1–4. Aune adds that the sayings that Sha'ul attributes to Yeshua in 1 Thessalonians 4:16–17a may have been reformulations of Yeshua's words or based on eschatological revelations he received directly from the Lord.[3]

4:3–12. What God wants is that you be holy, that you keep away from sexual immorality, that each of you know how to manage his sexual impulses in a holy and honorable manner, without giving in to lustful desires, like the pagans who do not know God. No one should wrong his brother in this matter or take advantage of him, because the Lord punishes all who do such things—as we have explained to you before at length. For God did not call us to live an unclean life but a holy one. Therefore, whoever rejects this teaching is rejecting not a man but God, indeed, the One who gives you the *Ruach HaKodesh*, which is his.

Sha'ul's instructions are reminiscent of the authoritative instructions given by the Jerusalem Council to non-Jewish believers (Acts 15:5) as well as "Paul's ethical summaries (e.g., Rom. 1:26–31;

2. William D. Davies, in *Paul and Rabbinic Judaism: Some Rabbinic Elements in Pauline Theology*, 141.
3. Aune, *Prophecy in Early Christianity*, 253–256.

48

13:13; 1 Cor. 5:1, 9–11; 6:9f.; 2 Cor. 12:20f.; Gal. 5:19-21; Col. 3:5, 8; 1 Thess. 4:1–8), which follow a common Hellenistic Jewish custom of summarizing the demands of the Torah by moral stipulations regarding idolatry, sexual misconduct, murder, avarice, etc."[4]

4:9–12. Concerning love for the brothers we do not need to write you, for you yourselves have been taught by God to love each other; and you do love all the brothers throughout Macedonia. But we urge you, brothers, to do it even more. Also, make it your ambition to live quietly, to mind your own business and to earn your living by your own efforts—just as we told you. Then your daily life will gain the respect of outsiders, and you will not be dependent on anyone.

These summaries were counterbalanced by the virtues that would effectively negate the conduct that was antithetical to the Torah.[5]

4:13–18 – Introduction

Muller describes these verses as "a prophetic proclamation of salvation for the purpose of consolation." [6] The Thessalonians fervently expected the *parousia* would relieve and rescue them from their suffering and would take place during their lifetime. When some of the members of their community passed away before that time, they grew dismayed and confused, so it was incumbent upon Sha'ul to clear up the misunderstandings and confusion. The Thessalonians needed further instructions and clarifications regarding the concept of the resurrection from the dead, which had been an integral element of his initial teaching when he came to Thessaloniki (Acts 17:1–3).

---

4. Bockmuehl, *Revelation and Mystery*, 155. (e.g., Ps-Phoc; Ps-Heraclitus 7; T12Patr passim; cf. Wisd 14:12–27; SibOr3:8–45; 4:31–34; etc.)
5. Hans Conzelmann, et al., *1 Corinthians: A Commentary on The First Epistle to the Corinthians*, 100–102.
6. Aune, *Prophecy in Early Christianity*, 253–262.

4:13–14. Now, brothers, we want you to know the truth about those who have died; otherwise, you might become sad the way other people do who have nothing to hope. For since we believe that Yeshua died and rose again, we also believe that in the same way God, through Yeshua, will take with him those who have died.

Sha'ul's explanation regarding the resurrection and its relationship to the *parousia* reflects an apocalyptic belief that was associated with Pharisaic messianism. Pharisaic messianism can be defined as:

> A hope for membership in an already existent heavenly kingdom to be brought from heaven by a suddenly appearing messiah: for general judgment in which the righteous should be acquitted and the wicked condemned; for resurrection of the body and a life everlasting for the righteous; for an endless age in which God and happiness should be supreme and enjoyed forever by those whom he had justified.[7]

Death, which Sha'ul designates as the last enemy (1 Cor. 15:27), was considered an enemy that could never be defeated. Sha'ul then midrashically applies allusions to various Scriptures that indicate Yeshua's death and resurrection have conquered death, the foe previously thought unconquerable (cp. Ps. 8:7[6 MT]; 15:32; Isa. 22:13, 25:8; 56:12; Hos. 13:14). God has placed all things, including death, under Yeshua's feet.

The concept of a suffering Messiah is well-attested in Jewish literature. In a similar manner to John 19:37 and Revelation 1:7, the Sages understood Zachariah 12:10— "the one who was pierced"—as applying to a suffering Messiah, namely Messiah son of Joseph (Sukkah 52a). The belief in the suffering Messiah son of Joseph who is followed by the conquering Messiah son of David already existed

---

7. https://www.jstor.org/stable/3137007. 189.

during the time of Judas Maccabaeus (167–160 B.C.E.). The popular apocalyptic Book of Enoch (90:37–38), which speaks of the Messiah son of David and the Messiah son of Joseph, was well-known during the time of the Maccabees.[8] Yeshua is the suffering servant who is depicted in Isaiah 53.[9] The sacrifice of the *Mashiach* was vicarious (Isa. 53:4–6, 8b–10). He was buried (Isa. 53:9) and resurrected (Isa. 53:11–12). And, like the prophet Jonah being in the belly of a great fish, the *Mashiach* remained in the grave for three days and three nights (Mt. 12:40).

The resurrection of the righteous and the wicked on the Day of the Lord is referred to in Daniel 12:1–3 and heralds the arrival of the Messianic era:[10]

> "When that time comes, Mikha'el, the great prince who champions your people, will stand up; and there will be a time of distress unparalleled between the time they became a nation and that moment. At that time, your people will be delivered, everyone whose name is found written in the book. Many of those sleeping in the dust of the earth will awaken, some to everlasting life and some to everlasting shame and abhorrence. But those who can discern will shine like the brightness of heaven's dome, and those who turn many to righteousness like the stars forever and ever.

4:15–18. When we say this, we base it on the Lord's own word: we who remain alive when the Lord comes will certainly not take precedence over those who have died. For the Lord himself will come down from heaven with a rousing cry, with a call from one of

---

8. David Flusser, *Judaism and the Origins of Christianity*, 424.

9. Samuel Rolles Driver, *The "Suffering Servant" of Isaiah According to the Jewish Interpreters*.

10. Judah J. Slotki, Ephraim Oratz, and Shalom Shahar, *Daniel; Ezra; Nehemiah: Hebrew Text & English Translation*, 101.

the ruling angels, and with God's *shofar*; those who died united with the Messiah will be the first to rise; then we who are left still alive will be caught up with them in the clouds to meet the Lord in the air; and thus we will always be with the Lord. So, encourage each other with these words.

Sha'ul once again refers to direct revelations he received from Yeshua (1 Thess. 1:2; cf. 1 Cor. 11:23), which he transmits to the Thessalonians.

The Hebraic concept of transmitting divinely given instructions from one generation to another is known as *mesorah*. It is the careful chain of oral transmission of Jewish religious truth and/or tradition. Theologically, Orthodox Jews believe Moshe (Moses) received the Torah and each of its commandments (*mitzvos*) as well as their oral commentary from G-d. The oral traditions include not only the correct interpretation of the Torah but also the acceptable principles for leading a godly life. Tremendous care was taken to ensure that even the smallest detail was transmitted correctly. [11] This foundational belief is clearly delineated in the first *mishnah* of *Pirkei Avot*.

> *Moshe Rabbeinu* received the Torah from *Har Sinai* and transmitted it to Yehoshua, and Yehoshua to the Elders, and the Elders to the Prophets, and the Prophets transmitted it to the Men of the Great Assembly.[12]

Several verses in the *Brit Chadashah* indicate Sha'ul affirmed the practice of *mesorah*, meaning he transmitted to his *talmidim* that

---

11. For a more detailed explanation regarding the concept of *Mesorah*, please read "Mesorah: The Chain of Tradition," Torah.org, May 17, 2019, https://torah.org/learning/basics-primer-torah-mesora.

12. Avot 1:1 מֹשֶׁה קִבֵּל תּוֹרָה מִסִּינַי, וּמְסָרָהּ לִיהוֹשֻׁעַ, וִיהוֹשֻׁעַ לִזְקֵנִים, וּזְקֵנִים לִנְבִיאִים, וּנְבִיאִים מְסָרוּהָ לְאַנְשֵׁי כְנֶסֶת הַגְּדוֹלָה

which was revealed to him by the Lord, exclusive of the oral Traditions of the Elders.

God's Shofar

The eternal victory over the enemy death will be announced by the final sounding of the shofar (Isa. 27:13; Zech. 9:14; Mt. 24:31; 1 Thess. 4:16; Rev. 8:2). The phrase "on that day" (*bah yom ha-hu*, Isa. 27:13) is a technical term for "the last days."

> [13] On that day a great *shofar* will sound.
> Those lost in the land of Ashur will come,
> also those scattered through the land of Egypt;
> and they will worship *ADONAI*
> on the holy mountain in *Yerushalayim*.

4.17. Caught up with them in the clouds,

This is a reference to Matthew 24:30, which is based on Daniel 7:13. Geza Vermes states that in Jewish literature the cloud was considered to be a means of heavenly transport; a prime example can be found in a fragmentary Targum on Exodus 12:42, where it is written that King Messiah led Moses on the top of a cloud.[13] In a related comment, David Flusser remarks that according to Fifth Esdras, the future Jerusalem will be the dwelling place of the gentile believers who will be **gathered up** with Abraham, Isaac and Jacob and the prophets from the old dispensation.[14]

> The concept of "assumption," "translation," or "taking up" as God's way of bringing the righteous, especially unique individuals, into his company at death was commonplace in apocalyptic literature. The assumption of Enoch is described in Gen. 5:24 LXX and more overtly in 1 Enoch (70.1–71.17), the

---

13. Géza Vermès, *Jesus the Jew: A Historian's Reading of the Gospels*, 186–187.
14. Fluusser, *Judaism and the Origins*, 568.

assumption of Baruch in 2 Baruch (46.7), the assumption of Ezra in 4 Ezra (= 2 Esd. 14:9), and the assumption of Moses in" "Philo's Life of Moses (2.291). Similar examples occur elsewhere in both Jewish and early Christian writings. According to some texts, at death the soul is summoned to heaven and receives its judgment there (T. Ab. 1.7; 7.7; 17.3; 1 En. 22.9–14; LAB 23.13; cf. 33.3). Paul uses the term *harpazein* in 2 Cor. 12:2, 4 to describe his journey to the third heaven. In Greco-Roman literature, ascent of the deceased into heaven is described in terms of apotheosis: the soul, or rather the "divine" portion of the person, escapes the body and is "translated" into the heavenly region of the universe in the form of a comet. This is said to have been the fate of Julius Caesar (Vergil, *Aen.* 1.290; Suetonius, *Jul.* 88; Ovid, *Metam.* 15.745–870). In Lucian's satirical history A True Story (*Vera historia*), a certain Endymion is said to have been "raptured" (*anarpastheiē*) to the moon.[15]

4.18. So, encourage each other with these words.

The remedy for the Thessalonians' anxiety and discouragement is the reality of the resurrection from the dead.

---

15. Timothy A. Brookins, *First and Second Thessalonians*, 132.

First Thessalonians
Chapter Five

Introductory Remarks

The principal subject of these verses is the Day of the Lord.

W. D. Davies points out that in this chapter Sha'ul interweaves the words of Yeshua in the following verses: 5:2 with Matthew 24:43–44; 5:13 with Mark 9:50; and 5:15 with Matthew 5:39–47.[1]

U. B. Müller designates verses 1-11 as a proclamation of the "immanence of the eschaton as a part of the prophetic speech of admonition."[2]

5:1. But you have no need to have anything written to you, brothers, about the times and dates when this will happen;

The Hebrew concept of time in relationship to eschatological events is not concerned about a specific fixed date; rather its focus is the specific events that will occur at that time.

Meir Weiss, in his article "The Origin of the 'Day of the Lord'—Reconsidered," writes this about the Hebrew concept of time:

> Research in this field has shown time and again that: "The time of the action, which for us is the principal thing, is of no importance to the Hebrew. The Hebrew concept of 'time' is closely coincident with that of its content. Time is the notion of the occurrence; it is the stream of events." Thus, the concept "Day of the Lord" comes to indicate occurrence rather than the time.[3]

---

1. W. D. Davies, *Jewish and Pauline Studies*, 114.
2. Aune, *Prophecy in Early Christianity*, 262.
3. Weiss, 46–47.

That is why no man knows the Day or the hour unless God reveals it to him (Dan. 2:20–23; Mt. 24:36). The Day of the Lord will occur on a future unspecified day. Therefore, knowing the exact day and time is not essential. However, the following are some of the events that will occur on the Day of the Lord.

> On that day a great *shofar* will sound.
> Those lost in the land of Ashur will come,
> also those scattered through the land of Egypt;
> and they will worship *Adonai*
> on the holy mountain in *Yerushalayim*.
> Isaiah 27:13

> "In that day, the mountains will drip new wine,
> and the hills will flow with milk;
> all the ravines of Judah will run with water.
> A fountain will flow out of the Lord's house
> and will water the valley of acacias.
> Joel 3:18 (4:18 Hebrew)

> The Lord will be king over the whole earth.
> On that day there will be one Lord, and his name the only name.
> Zechariah 14:9

5:2a. The Day of the Lord

Though the expression "the Day of the Lord" appears 29 times in the *Tanakh*, according to Weiss, "In the light of the relevant data, it seems plausible, though not proven, that the phrase 'Day of the Lord' was coined by Amos who uses it for the first time in his prophecy (Amos 5:18–20). This would imply that Amos' audience heard this expression for the first time from this prophecy. But in the light of the concepts of 'time' and 'day' in Hebrew it would appear that even though the designation was not familiar to the audience of Amos they understood its meaning."[4]

> Woe to you who want the Day of *ADONAI*!
> Why do you want it, this Day of *ADONAI*?
> It is darkness, not light;
> as if someone were to run from a lion,
> just to be met by a bear;
> as if he entered a house, put his hand on the wall,
> just to be bitten by a snake.
> Won't the Day of *ADONAI* be darkness, not light,
> completely dark, with no brightness at all?
> Amos 5:18–20

Daniella Ishai-Rosenboim, in her article "Is 'the Day of the Lord' a Term in Biblical Language?" characterizes the Day of the Lord as the day of torment, the day of Judgment, the day of tumult and curse and wrath and anger.[5]

The *Jewish Annotated New Testament*, in its comments on 1 Thessalonians 1:5–11, offers the following insights concerning the phrase:

> Paul instructs the Thessalonians how to prepare for the day of the Lord, a phrase appearing often in the Prophets (e.g., Isa. 2.12–17; Joel 2.1; Amos 5.18, 20; Zep. 1.7), who use it to describe divine action including: God's retribution against foreign nations that oppressed Israel; God's punishment of Israel, Judah, or the Jewish people, and vindication of the oppressed; God's reestablishment of Israel, Judah or the Jewish people under the

---

4 . Meir Weiss, "The Origin of the 'Day of the Lord' – Reconsidered." https://www.jstor.org/stable/23503114.

5. Y. Hoffman, "Is יוֹם ה (the Day of the Lord) a Term in Biblical Language?" https://www.jstor.org/stable/42614691.

rule and justice of God. Some texts specifically mention a messiah or Davidic king (e.g., Jer. 23.5–6; Amos 9.11) while others include the redemption of Gentile nations or all creation (e.g., Isa. 2.2–4; Mic. 4.1–3). New Testament writers use it, or variations of it (e.g., 1 Cor. 1.8; 5.5; 2 Tim. 1.18; Heb. 9.28; 10.5), to refer to Jesus' return.[6]

It is interesting to note that here is a Jewish tradition that there will be great suffering before the advent of the Messiah. We are thus taught, "One third of the world's woes will come in the generation preceding the Messiah."[7]

In my estimation, the *parousia* is conglomeration of interrelated, sequential, or simultaneous events that are included in the "Day of the Lord."

5:2b. Will come

Sha'ul not only associates the *parousia* with an official visit from Caesar, but by using the Greek *erchomai* ("to come")[8] he also associates the *parousia* with a bridegroom (*Chatan*) returning for his bride (*Kalah*). In the New Testament, *erchomai* is frequently used in such a context, including the Parable of the Ten Maidens, commonly known as the Parable of the Wise and Foolish Virgins (Mt. 25:1–13). Yeshua's promise to return for his "Bride" after he has prepared a place for her in his father's house is found in John 14:1–3. Samuel Tobias Lachs says, "If the bridegroom is God, then the motif is common in rabbinic sources. The best illustration is the one in which Moses wakens Israel by saying, "The Bridegroom is coming" (*Pirqe*

---

6. Amy-Jill Levine, *Jewish Annotated New Testament*, 376–377.
7. Rabbi Aryeh Kaplan, "The Pre-Messianic Era," from *Handbook of Jewish Thought*. https://aish.com/48931432.
8. The word-group includes 77 unique forms.

de-Rabbi Eliezer).[9] *Erchomai* is also associated with the bride's invitation to attend the marriage feast.

First-century Jewish wedding customs were comprised of two major sections: *erusin* (betrothal) and *nissuin* (marriage). After the betrothal, the groom would go to his father's house to prepare a place for his bride. It was the sole discretion of the groom's father to determine the time and the season that his son, the groom, could return to his bride to take her to his father's house. This is what Yeshua in his capacity of groom meant when he said, "But when that day and hour will come, no one knows—not the angels in heaven, not the Son, only the Father" (Mt. 24:36).

When the groom did return, his arrival was announced with the sound of the shofar. The bride was lifted up into a bridal palanquin (wedding litter) and brought by the wedding attendants to the groom's residence, his father's house, where the second part of the marriage ceremony (*nissuin*) took place. The ceremony was followed by a seven-day wedding feast.[10] Yeshua's wedding feast is known as the Marriage Supper of the Lamb (Rev. 19:6–9).

Kevin D. Zuber, in his commentary on 1 Thessalonians, agrees that the *parousia* is like a bridegroom, coming to retrieve his bride in fulfillment of Yeshua's promise in John 14:1–3 to take his bride to his Father's house, where the wedding feast will complete the formal union of marriage (cf. Rev. 9:7–9).[11]

Matthew's version of Synoptic Apocalypse interweaves *parousia* with *erchomai*, demonstrating the two words are parallel expressions

---

9. Lachs, *A Rabbinic Commentary*, 391.

10. For further information, see Jamie Lash, *The Ancient Jewish Wedding: And the Return of Messiah for His Bride*.

11 . Michael Rydelnik and Michael G. Vanlaningham, *The Moody Bible Commentary*.

that refer to Yeshua's appearance at the End of Days (Mt. 24:27,39 – *parousia*; 24:30,42 – *erchomai*).

5:2c. A thief in the night

Thieves come under the cover of darkness while people are sleeping. That is why believers should not spiritually fall asleep. This is also an allusion to Matthew 24:43–44 and Song of Songs 5:2.

> I am asleep, but my heart is awake.
> Listen! I hear my darling knocking!
>
> Open for me, my sister, my love,
> my dove, my flawless one!
> For my head is wet with dew,
> my hair with the moisture of the night.
> Song of Solomon 5:2

5:3a. When people are saying, "Everything is so peaceful and secure," then destruction will suddenly come upon them.

To show the believers where their true security lay, Sha'ul attacks the *Pax et Securitas* (peace and security), the watchwords of the *Pax Romana*. He condemned the existing world system, which was indifferent to the coming of the Lord.[12]

5:3b. Labor pains come upon a pregnant woman

Chevlai HaMashiach or the birth pains of the Messiah is a Jewish prophetic term that is associated with the Day of the Lord and is first found in Jeremiah 30:4–7 (cf. Mt. 24:8):

These are the words *ADONAI* spoke concerning Isra'el and Y'hudah:

---

12 . Robert I. Bradshaw, "The Purposes Behind Paul's First Epistle to the Thessalonians," January 1, 1990, https://www.biblicalstudies.org.uk/article_1thess.html.

Here is what *ADONAI* says:
"We have heard a cry of terror,
of fear and not of peace.
Ask now and see:
can men give birth to children?
Why, then, do I see all the men
with their hands on their stomachs like women in labor,
with every face turned pale?
How dreadful that day will be!—
there has never been one like it:
a time of trouble for Ya'akov,
but out of it he will be saved.
Jeremiah 30:4–7

5:5. For you are all people who belong to the light, who belong to the day. We do not belong to the night or to darkness.

Believers are the Sons of Light, while unbelievers are the Sons of Darkness (Jn. 1:4–5, 8–9; 3:19–21; 12:36; 1 John 1:5–8).

The community at Qumran expresses a similar idea in *The War Scroll*, also called *The War of the Sons of Light Against the Sons of Darkness*. This document speaks of the final eschatological battle between Belial, leading the Sons of Darkness, and the archangel Michael, leading the Sons of Light.[13]

The apparent purpose of *The War Scroll* was to give the members of the Essene community at Qumran a detailed set of regulations for the day destined from eternity for a battle of annihilation of the Sons of Darkness by the Sons of Light. The result of this war is pre-ordained; God himself will intervene on the side of the Sons of Light. Yet this intervention will take place only after a

---

13 . Michael Edward Stone, *Jewish Writings of the Second Temple Period: Apocrypha, Pseudepigrapha, Qumran Sectarian Writings, Philo, Josephus*, 340.

series of real battles in which the Sons of Darkness will alternately be defeated and victorious. The war will have to be fought according to all the rules of war practiced by the nations, but also in accordance with the Law of Moses.[14]

5:8. Putting on trust and love as a breastplate and the hope of being delivered as a helmet

This is a direct reference to Isaiah 59:17, where God is represented as a warrior whose weapons consist of righteousness, salvation, vengeance and zeal, attributes used for the chastisement of the wicked and the deliverance of the godly.[15] The context of verse 19 is the appearance at the end of days of a Redeemer who will come to Zion that will fill the children and descendants of *Ya'akov* with the Spirit of *Adonoi.*

> *ADONAI* saw it, and it displeased him
> that there was no justice.
> He saw that there was no one,
> was amazed that no one interceded.
> Therefore his own arm brought him salvation,
> and his own righteousness sustained him.
> He put on righteousness as his breastplate,
> salvation as a helmet on his head;
> he clothed himself with garments of vengeance
> and wrapped himself in a mantle of zeal.
> He repays according to their deeds—
> fury to his foes, reprisal to his enemies;
> to the coastlands he will repay their due;

---

14. Stone, *Jewish Writings*, 515.
15. I. W. Slotki and A. J. Rosenberg, *Isaiah: Hebrew Text & English Translation,* 291.

in the west they will fear the name of *ADONAI*,
and likewise, in the east, his glory.

For he will come like a pent-up stream,
impelled by the Spirit of *ADONAI*.
"Then a Redeemer will come to Tziyon,
to those in Ya'akov who turn from rebellion."
So says *ADONAI*.
"And as for me," says *ADONAI*,
"this is my covenant with them:
my Spirit, who rests on you,
and my words which I put in your mouth
will not depart from your mouth
or from the mouth of your children,
or from the mouth of your children's children,
now or ever," says *ADONAI*.
Isaiah 59:15b–21

Believers are to figuratively clothe themselves with God's armor. A parallel expression is found in Ephesians 6:10–20.

5:9. For God has not intended that we should experience his fury

The Day of the Lord is the time when his enemies will experience his fury and final judgment. The Sages describe what will happen when God judges the earth:

> Rabbi Yitzchak said that Rabbi Yochanan said, "In the generation when the Son of David is to come, scholars will be few. As for others, their eyes will fail from sorrow and grief. There will be much trouble, and evil decrees will be renewed, with each new evil coming quickly, even before the other has ended." Our Rabbis taught that the following would happen during the seven years at the end of which the Son of David is to come. In the first year, "I will cause it to rain upon one city and cause it not to rain upon another city" (Amos 4:7). In the second, the arrows of

hunger will be sent forth [food shortages, with no one being fully satisfied]. In the third, there will be a great famine, during which men, women, children, pious men, and saints will die; and [hunger will cause] the Torah to be forgotten by its *talmidim*. In the fourth, there will be surpluses of some things but shortages of others. In the fifth there will be great plenty—people will eat, drink, and rejoice; and the Torah will return to its *talmidim*. In the sixth year, there will be sounds [in the light of what follows, either rumors of wars (compare Mt. 24:6) or heavenly voices or shofar blasts (see 8:2N) announcing the Messiah's coming]. In the seventh year there will be wars. And at the end of the seven years the Son of David will come. (Sanhedrin 97a)[16]

God had previously poured out his wrath on the enemies of his people, the prime example being the events associated with the Exodus from Egypt, the paradigm being Pharaoh and the Egyptians representing the sons of darkness and Moses and the children of Israel representing the sons of light. Yeshua, like Moses, is the Redeemer of his people, and his redemptive act symbolizes freedom from the slavery of sin. His death and resurrection and the proclamation of the gospel is the inciting incident that sets in motion the eschatological realization of the wrath of God and the imminent appearance of the Son of Man coming on the clouds of glory to establish the Kingdom of God.

God's wrath is a fate from which the Thessalonians have been delivered (1 Thess. 1.10, 5.9) and is reserved for their opponents (2.16; 2 Thess. 1.6–9; 2.10–12).[17]

5:10. We should gain deliverance through our Lord Yeshua the Messiah

---

16. Stern, *Jewish New Testament Commentary*, 72.
17. I. Howard Marshall and Karl P. Donfried, *New Testament Theology: The Theology of the Shorter Pauline Letters*.

Yeshua is Lord (*Kurios*), also a title claimed by Caesar. Sha'ul wants the Thessalonians to know that only Yeshua, not Caesar, can bring everlasting peace and deliverance.

5:12–18. We ask you, brothers, to respect those who are working hard among you, those who are guiding you in the Lord and confronting you to help you change. Treat them with the highest regard and love because of the work they are doing. Live at peace among yourselves; but we urge you, brothers, to confront those who are lazy, your aim being to help them change, to encourage the timid, to assist the weak, and to be patient with everyone. See that no one repays evil for evil; on the contrary, always try to do good to each other, indeed, to everyone. Always be joyful. Pray regularly. In everything give thanks, for this is what God wants from you who are united with the Messiah Yeshua.

In these verses Sha'ul presents an extensive list of what constitutes responsible behavior such as respecting leaders, supporting and encouraging one another, and incessant prayer. Life's true victories are won by believers who are joyful, prayerful, and thankful.[18] Verse 5:15 is a reference to Matthew 5:38–48.

5:19-21. Do not quench the Spirit, don't despise inspired messages. But do test everything—hold onto what is good but keep away from every form of evil.

From the beginning of this letter and through its conclusion, Sha'ul emphasizes and unfolds the key role of the work of the *Ruach HaKodesh*. The Spirit is active in the preaching and reception of the gospel (1.5f). His presence is associated with power and joy (1.5f). He is God's gift to believers (4.8) and is associated with holiness;

---

18. Gaebelein, *Expositor's Bible Commentary*, 291.

one must beware of disregarding the Spirit by lapsing into sin. Spiritual gifts, such as prophecy, must not be quenched (5.19).[19]

In his letters Sha'ul emphasizes that inspired messages (prophecy) were a normative congregational activity (Rom. 12:6; 1 Cor. 12:10, 28–29; 14:6, 22, 29–33). He reminds the Thessalonians that during the Messianic Age, God promised he would pour out his *Ruach* on "all Flesh" and they would prophesy (Joel 2:28–29 (3:1–2),[20] a process that began on Shavuot (Acts 2:17–18).

5:23–28. May the God of *shalom* make you completely holy—may your entire spirit, soul and body be kept blameless for the coming of our Lord Yeshua the Messiah. The one calling you is faithful, and he will do it. Brothers, keep praying for us. Greet all the brothers with a holy kiss. I charge you in the Lord to have this letter read to all the brothers. The grace of our Lord Yeshua the Messiah be with you.

Sha'ul reiterates the importance of being prepared "blameless"— spirit, soul, and body—for the *parousia* of the Lord Yeshua. "Spirit, soul and body" can be understood as a paraphrase of Deuteronomy 6:5, which says, "You shall love the Lord your God with all your heart (spirit), with all your being (soul), and with all your resources (body)" (cf. Mt. 22:37; Mk. 12:30).

19. Marshall and Donfried, *New Testament Theology*.
20. A. Cohen, *The Twelve Prophets*, 72.

ADDENDA

"Was Paul Anti-Semitic?
Revisiting 1 Thessalonians 2:14–16"[1]

By Michael A. Rydelnik,
Professor of Jewish Studies, Moody Bible Institute, Chicago, Illinois

A few years ago, Mel Gibson's *The Passion of the Christ* incited fears that the movie would awaken dormant Christian anti-Semitism. In fact, when the movie premiered, several newspapers and a national newsmagazine ran a photograph of a sign in front of a church that partially quoted 1 Thessalonians 2:14–15: "The Jews … killed the Lord Jesus."

These verses have long been considered a thorny passage for Jewish-Christian relations because they blame the Jewish people uniquely for the death of Yeshua. The Christ-killer accusation, historically a frequent basis for anti-Semitism, is known as the "deicide charge." It alleges that all Jews are guilty of killing Yeshua, and 1 Thessalonians 2:14–16 is cited as a basis for Christian anti-Semitism.

Paul wrote, "For you, brethren, became imitators of the churches of God in Christ Jesus that are in Judea, for you also endured the same sufferings at the hands of your own countrymen, even as they did from the Jews, who both killed the Lord Jesus and the prophets, and drove us out. They are not pleasing to God but hostile to all men, hindering us from speaking to the Gentiles so that they may be saved; with the result that they always fill up the measure of their sins. But wrath has come upon them to the utmost."

---

1. *Bibliotheca Sacra*, Volume 165:657 (Jan. 2008). Used by permission.

Best evaluated 1 Thessalonians 2:14–16 and concluded that it "shows Paul holding an unacceptable anti-Semitic position."[2] The problem with this passage is that it contradicts Paul's loving attitude toward the Jewish people found in Romans 9–11.

More specifically, as noted above, verse 15 seems to uphold the deicide charge, in apparent contradiction to the historical record of the Gospels[3] and Acts 4:27–28. This article examines and evaluates several attempts to deal with these difficulties and then proposes a solution.

Traditional Interpretation

The traditional view of these words is that they are Paul's blanket condemnation of the unbelieving Jewish nation. Denney writes, "It is vehement condemnation, by a man in a thorough sympathy with the mind and spirit of God, of the principles on which the Jews as a nation had acted at every period of their history."[4] Morris attempts to harmonize this with Romans 9–11 by saying these words express Paul's anguish for his nation, though his sorrow is not mitigated by any hope.[5]

Regarding the phrase "the Jews who both killed the Lord Jesus and the prophets" and its apparent contradiction to Acts 4:27–28 and the historical accounts of the Gospels, Hiebert expresses the

---

2 . Ernest Best, *A Commentary on the First and Second Epistles to the Thessalonians*, 122.

3. Matthew 27:25 ("And all the people said, 'His blood shall be on us and on our children'") has frequently been cited to show the Gospels also blamed the Jewish people for the death of Jesus. However, this misreads the point of the passage and the overall historical record. See Michael A. Rydelnik, "His Blood Be Upon Us," *Mishkan* 6/7 (1987): 1–9.

4. James Denney, *The Epistles to the Thessalonians* of *An Exposition of the Bible*, 330.

5 . Leon Morris, *The First and Second Epistles to the Thessalonians*, New *International Commentary on the New Testament*, 92.

traditional view. "It is interesting to note that in this epistle, written about twenty years after the crucifixion of Yeshua, Paul places the guilt for his death squarely upon the Jews. He was well aware that the execution was carried out by the Romans, that Pontius Pilate and Herod Antipas shared responsibility for that monumental miscarriage of justice (1 Cor. 2:8), but he saw clearly that the Jews were chiefly responsible, using Pilate as their tool to bring about the death of the one they hated."[6]

To summarize, the traditional interpretation of 1 Thessalonians 2:14–16 says these verses contain a blanket condemnation of the Jews as a nation. They are not in contradiction with Romans 9–11 because they reflect a cry of anguish (without any hope) as well as a shout of anger. They teach that the Jews as a nation are chiefly responsible for the death of Yeshua, and for this reason Paul was not contradicting Acts 4:27–28 and the historical record. This view holds that Paul was condemning the guiltiest group.

The traditional interpretation falls short for several reasons. First, in Romans, Paul did not express any harsh condemnation of the Jews. Instead, he expressed great sorrow and love for them (9:1–3; 10:1). Second, no note of anguish is in 1 Thessalonians 2:14–16. Moreover, in Romans he did express great hope for the future salvation of Israel (11:12, 25–27). Third, though Caiaphas had greater guilt in the crucifixion than Pilate (John 19:11), no New Testament passage says that the Jews as a nation were more guilty. In his address to the Pisidian Jews, Paul did not condemn the whole nation for this misdeed. Instead, he blamed the leaders and their Jerusalem supporters (Acts 13:27–28).

---

6. D. Edmond Hiebert, *The Thessalonian Epistles*, 115. William Hendriksen uses this verse to condemn Jewish people for Jesus' death, not only first-century Jews but all Jews since then who have not believed (*Israel in Prophecy*, 9).

Two Alternative Interpretations

Recognizing that the traditional view fails to account for all the New Testament data, other approaches have been proposed.

A Non-Pauline Interpolation

The difficulty in this passage caused Bauer to doubt the authenticity of the entire letter.[7] Viewing this approach as too radical, other critical scholars offer the view that only this section is non-Pauline.[8] By placing the pen in the hand of a later interpolator, it is thought that the alleged anti-Semitism of the passage is easily handled.[9]

Pearson offers several arguments against Pauline authorship of the passage. First, he cites the seemingly abrupt nature of the passage in relation to the argument of the epistle.[10] Second, he says the verses commend the example of the Judean church, whereas it was Paul's habit to commend the imitation of himself (1 Cor. 4:16; 11:1; Phil. 3:17) and through him the imitation of Christ (1 Cor. 11:1; 1 Thess. 1:6), never the imitation of a church.[11] Third, he argues the passage leans heavily on Matthew 23:31–36,[12] which was written

---

7. F. C. Bauer, *Paul the Apostle of Jesus Christ*, trans. A. Menzies, 87–88.

8. For example, Pearson, "1 Thessalonians 2:13–16," 79–94; and Hendrikus Boers, "The Form Critical Study of Paul's Letters: 1 Thessalonians as 'A Case Study,' " *New Testament Studies* 22 (1976): 40–58. James Moffatt regarded only 2:16c as a later insertion ("The First and Second Epistles to the Thessalonians" in *The Expositior's Greek Testament*, ed. W. Robertson Nicoll, 4:29. Surprisingly, F. F. Bruce leans toward this view. "Unless he changed his mind radically on this subject in the interval of seven years between the writing of I Thessalonians and of Romans, it is difficult to make him responsible for the viewpoint expressed here" (*1 and 2 Thessalonians – Word Biblical Commentary*, 48–49).

9. James Parkes, *The Conflict of the Church and the Synagogue*, 52; and Clark Williamson, *Has God Rejected His People?*, 63.

10. Pearson, "1 Thessalonians 2:13–16," 89–91.

11. Ibid., 87–88.

12. Ibid., 92.

later than the epistle. Fourth, he maintains that the mention of wrath (1 Thess. 2:16) refers to A.D. 70, when Jerusalem was destroyed, and so this paragraph, he argues, would postdate the rest of the epistle.[13] Pearson also cites the theological conflict with Romans 9–11 and the attribution of guilt for killing Christ as arguments favoring a deutero-Pauline interpolation.[14]

Several responses may be given to these objections.[15] First, as to the abrupt style, Best remarks, "v. 17 admittedly does not fit well after v. 16 but it fits no better after v. 12."[16] Furthermore, it is characteristic for Paul to be diverted from his main subject into a brief polemic (e.g., Phil. 3:1–6). Second, it is wrong to say Paul never commended a church as an example to other believers, for in 1 Thessalonians 1:7 he cited the Thessalonians themselves as an example to all the churches in Macedonia and Achaia.[17] Third, dependence on Matthew 23:31–36 need not negate Pauline authorship. Some scholars posit an early date for Matthew (ca. 44 A.D.),[18] and if this is accepted, it is feasible Paul could have been aware of it. If the date for Matthew was later, it is possible Paul was aware of the same source Matthew used. Fourth, the wrath spoken of in 1 Thessalonians 2:16 need not argue against Pauline authenticity. Paul may have had the

---

13. Ibid., 82–83.

14. Ibid., 85–86.

15. For an article that critiques this view, see J. Coppens, "Une Diatribe Antique dans 1 Thessalonians 2:13–16, " *Ephemeridum Theologia Lovaniensium Leuven* 51 (May 1976): 90–95. Best also defends the integrity of this paragraph (*A Commentary on the 1st and 2nd Epistles to the Thessalonians*, 123).

16. Best, *A Commentary*, 123.

17. Coppens, "Une Diatribe Antique dans 1 Thessalonians 2:13–16, " 92.

18 . David Alan Black summarizes Bernard Orchard's arguments for giving Matthew priority and dating it before 44 A.D. (*Why Four Gospels?*, 234). For a good discussion in support of an early date see R. H. Gundry, *Matthew: A Commentary on His Literary and Theological Art*, 599–608. For the most cogent arguments regarding the priority of Matthew over Luke and Mark, see William R. Farmer, *The Synoptic Problem*, 233–83.

coming judgment in view, using the aorist verb ἔφθασεν (*ephthasen*) proleptically.[19] As to the apparent contradiction with the rest of the Pauline writings, this assumes no other satisfactory solution can be found. If there is a suitable harmonization, this objection is removed. Also, there is no textual evidence suggesting these verses were interpolated.[20] Thus, there is no compelling reason to take 2:14–16 as a Deutero-Pauline interpolation.

An Early Outburst

Also proposed is to see 1 Thessalonians 2:14–16 as an emotional outburst by Paul before he formulated his well-developed theology in Romans 9–11.[21]

Three arguments are given in support of this view. First, it is suggested that Paul was using some traditionally formulated materials that contained an anti-Jewish bias. Later on, when Paul thought through the matter, he rejected these ideas.[22] Second, Best suggests an unknown outrage from an unknown Jewish source prompted Paul to vary from the outlook that characterizes his later writings.[23] Third, Baum explains Paul's words as an outburst cast in the mold of Hebrew prophets, castigating their own people in love. Baum sees this passage not as "an irreformable theological pronouncement,

---

19. James Everett Frame, *A Critical and Exegetical Commentary on the Epistles of St. Paul to the Thessalonians*, 114.
20. W. D. Davies, "Paul and the People of Israel," *New Testament Studies* 24 (1977): 6.
21. Ibid., 8; Williamson, *Has God Rejected His People?*, 63; Coppens, "Une Diatribe Antique dans 1 Thessalonians 2:13–16," 94; Best, *A Commentary*, 122; and Gregory Baum, *Is the New Testament Anti-Semitic?*, 293. Most recently this view has been defended by Donald Hagner, "Paul's Quarrel With Judaism," in *Anti-Semitism and Early Christianity*, ed. Craig Evans and Donald Hagner, 130–36.
22. Davies, "Paul and the People of Israel," 8; and Best, *A Commentary*, 122.
23. Best, *A Commentary*, 122.

but rather as a violent outburst of the anger and indignation which was the privilege of Jewish property."[24]

The following answers may be given against this view. First, the proposal that Paul used some traditionally formulated materials—and then later determined his words in 1 Thessalonians 2:14–16 was mistaken, so he wrote Romans 9–11 to correct them—takes a weak, contradictory view of the doctrine of inspiration. Second, the same can be said for the explanation derived from positing an intemperate reaction to an unknown expression of Jewish outrage. Is Paul's inscripturated outburst any less inerrant than Romans 9–11? Third, as to Paul's words being like those of Jewish prophets, recall that Hebrew prophets addressed their diatribes to their own nation, but Paul was writing to gentiles. Thus, it is safe to say that 1 Thessalonians 2:14–16 is not an early emotional outburst that Paul later corrected or softened.

A Proposed View

A more-plausible view is to see this passage in a narrow sense, condemning the Jewish leaders and their followers but not the Jews in general.[25] Several facts support this view. First, the persecution spoken of in 2:14 was interracial. Paul commended the Thessalonians because they were able to endure persecution at the hands of their "countrymen" even as the Jewish churches did at the hands of other Jews. The word συμφυλέτης, a *hapax legomenon*, is an ethnic term

---

24. Baum, *Is the New Testament Anti-Semitic?*, 293.

25. I. Howard Marshall follows Marxsen in holding this view (*The New Century Bible Commentary: 1 & 2 Thessalonians*, 82–83). This is similar to John's frequent use of the term "the Jews" to refer to the Jewish leaders (John 1:19, 24; 7:13; 9:22; 18:14). See Urban C. von Wahlde, "The Johannine 'Jews': A Critical Survey," *New Testament Studies* 28 (January 1982): 33–60. For a helpful explanation see F. F. Bruce, "Are the Gospels Anti-Semitic?" *Eternity* 1973, 16–18.

meaning "of the same tribe or race."[26] Thus, Paul was saying that unsaved gentiles were persecuting gentile Christians, and unsaved Jews were persecuting Jewish Christians. Therefore, Paul was not referring to *all* Jews since the passage includes some Jews (believers in Judea, v. 14) who did not take part in these sinful acts.

Second, the sins Paul said the Jews committed are limited in the Gospels to the Jewish leaders. The Gospels make clear that the Jewish leaders, not the entire Jewish nation, plotted Yeshua's death (Jn. 11:47–53), accused him before Pilate and Herod (Lk. 23:2, 10) and incited the crowd (Mt. 27:20; Mk. 15:11).

Third, the parable of the vine growers (Mt. 21:33–46; Mk. 12:1–12; Lk. 20:9–19) and the condemnation of the Pharisees (Mt. 23:29–36) demonstrate Paul was speaking of the Jewish leaders.[27] The same pattern occurs in each passage. In the parable the vineyard owner sent slave after slave, each of whom the vine growers murdered. Then the son was sent; he too was murdered. After Yeshua told the parable, the chief priests and Pharisees knew he was speaking of them as the ones who opposed him (Mt. 21:45–46; Mk. 12:12; Lk. 20:19).

---

26. H. G. Liddell and R. Scott, *An Intermediate Greek-English Lexicon*, 765. Most commentators recognize this means that the Thessalonian persecutors were Gentiles. However, the Jewish persecution in Thessalonica (Acts 17:5) leads some commentators to include Jews along with Gentiles in Paul's reference to the Thessalonians' "countrymen" (Best, *A Commentary*, 114; Morris, *First and Second Epistles*, 89; Hiebert, *The Thessalonian Epistles*, 113; and Moffatt, "The First and Second Epistles to the Thessalonians," 29). This is unfortunate, since the word συμφυλέτης is limited to people groups. Thus the συμφυλέτης of the Thessalonians were gentiles, and those of the Judeans were Jews. Perhaps Paul could refer to the Thessalonian persecutors this way because the Jews had already ceased their instigation. Those who correctly recognize the ethnic meaning of this word include Frame, *A Critical and Exegetical Commentary on the Epistles of St. Paul to the Thessalonians*, 110; Pearson, "1 Thessalonians 2:13–16," 886; A. T. Robertson, *Word Pictures in the New Testament*, 4:21; and Charles Ryrie, *First & Second Thessalonians*, 41.
27. J. B. Orchard, "Thessalonians and the Synoptic Gospels" *Biblica* 19 (1938), 19–42.

Yeshua called the Pharisees the sons of the prophets' murderers (Mt. 23:31), and he said they would persecute those he would send (v. 34). As a result, the full measure of their guilt would be evident (vv. 32, 35) and Jerusalem would be destroyed (v. 38).

The same pattern is found in 1 Thessalonians 2:14–16. The Jews who persecuted the Judean churches also murdered the prophets and the Messiah and persecuted his messengers. In doing this they filled up the full measure of their guilt, resulting in judgment. Since Yeshua himself specifically applied these things to the leaders of Israel, it is safe to say Paul was following the same pattern.

This view resolves the apparent contradiction with other Scriptures that mention responsibility for Yeshua's death. Paul was not indicting all Jews; he was indicting only the leaders and their henchmen.

Some may object that while Paul did not accuse all Jews, he did limit responsibility for Yeshua's death to the Jews. However, this is an argument from silence. Paul was not writing about human responsibility for Christ's death but about persecution of the Thessalonian believers. He was writing to encourage them in their suffering. He did so by pointing out that since "persecution had not brought the work of God to an end in the place of its origin and the home of its fiercest enemies, it would avail as little in Thessalonica."[28] Paul chose to speak of the Jewish leaders because they served as an illustration, not because they were solely responsible.

Thus, the seeming contradiction between Paul's position in 1 Thessalonians 2:14–16 and the rest of Scripture regarding human responsibility for the death of the Messiah is solved by limiting Paul's meaning of "the Jews" in that passage to the Jewish leaders.

---

28. C. F. Hogg and W. E. Vine, *The Epistles of Paul the Apostle to the Thessalonians*, 74.

Another problem is Paul's unusual word order in v. 15. He separated the nouns κύριον ("Lord") and Ἰησοῦν ("Jesus") by the participle ἀποκτεινάντων ("killed"), thus emphasizing κύριον. Hiebert interprets this stress as an indictment of the Jews for the murder of God: "It was none less than the exalted Lord whom the Jews killed ... his death at their hands was no common murder."[29]

Blinzler clearly answers the charge of deicide: "Much has been spoken of deicide [...] the New Testament makes no such reproach either to the Sanhedrin or to the procurator. Since the enemies of Yeshua lacked any deep insight into the mystery of His being, their act was not actually the crime of deicide."[30] Thus, it seems best to view Paul's stress on κύριον not as a condemnation of the Jews for deicide but as a statement of the nobility of Yeshua and the undeserved nature of his death.

The problem of harmonizing this passage with Romans 9–11 remains. The alleged contradiction stems from the fact that 1 Thessalonians 2:16 seems to teach an unending judgment on Israel, whereas Paul expressed glorious hope for Israel in Romans 11:26–27. What did he mean by the clause "φθασεν δ π᾽ α το ργ ε ς τέλος"?[31]

This sentence has five possible meanings. First, the aorist ἔφθασεν may be taken as a constative and the phrase ε ς τέλος may mean "forever." This would teach the *permanent rejection* of Israel.[32] But this is not correct since the very opposite is clearly taught in Romans 11:25–29.

A second possibility is to take ἔφθασεν constatively and translate εἰς τέλος as "uttermost." This would describe the intensity of the

---

29. Hiebert, *The Thessalonian Epistles*, 115.
30. J. Blinzler, *The Trial of Jesus*, trans. Isabel and Florence McHugh, 293.
31. *The New American Standard Bible* translates this, "but wrath has come upon them to the utmost"; the *NIV* renders it, "The wrath of God has come upon them at last."
32. Best, *A Commentary*,, 21.

wrath and refer to the *partial judicial blindness* of Israel.[33] However, Israel's blindness is not unique. All "natural" people—that is, those who have not trusted in Yeshua—are spiritually blind (cf. 1 Cor. 2:14). It is incorrect to view the blindness of Israel as a special or unique judicial blindness. Instead, theirs is the normal spiritual blindness that results from unbelief.[34]

A third suggestion is that the aorist ἔφθασεν is constative and that εἰς τέλος means "finally." Together they refer to *some tragedy* that occurred a brief time before Paul wrote (e.g., Claudius's expulsion of Jews from Rome 49 A.D., the famine in 46 or 47, the insurrection of Theudas, or some unknown tragedy).[35] However, it seems that something more tragic is in view here.

Fourth, it is possible to see the aorist ἔφθασεν proleptically and ε ς τέλος as "in the end," thereby referring to *eschatological judgment*.[36] However, Paul emphasized eschatological blessing, not judgment, for Israel (Rom. 11:12, 26).

Fifth, it is possible to take the aorist ἔφθασεν proleptically and the words ε ς τέλος as "finally." The clause would then be translated "wrath will finally come on them" (cf. NIV), with the words referring prophetically to *the destruction of Jerusalem,* which was to happen in 70 A.D.[37] This is parallel to Matthew 23, in which Yeshua concluded his condemnation of the Pharisees with a reference to Jerusalem's then-future destruction. Moreover, since the leaders' rejection of Yeshua caused the judgment (cf. Luke 19:41–44), it

33. William Hendriksen, *Exposition of First and Second Thessalonians*, 73.
34. Amado Lozano, "The Present Outworking of the Abrahamic Covenant as Evidenced Through the Concept of the Remnant" (Th.M. thesis, Dallas Theological Seminary, 1982, 46–47).
35. Best, *A Commentary*, 120.
36. F. F. Bruce, "1 and 2 Thessalonians," in *The New Bible Commentary: Revised*, ed. Donald Guthrie, et al., 1157; Morris, *1 and 2 Thessalonians*, 92; and Best, *A Commentary*, 120.
37. Orchard, "Thessalonians and the Synoptic Gospels," 19–42.

seems likely Paul would have referred to the same idea after discussing the leaders' involvement in Yeshua's death. This view easily harmonizes with Romans 9–11, having a specific judgment in view. When God's wrath fell in 70 A.D., the specific judgment for the nation's rejection of the Messiah through her leaders was completed.[38] Nothing in Romans 9–11 contradicts this.

Thus, the statement in 1 Thessalonians 2:14–16 is a limited condemnation. Paul was speaking of a specific group, the Jewish leaders, whose rejection of Yeshua as Messiah resulted in a specific judgment, the destruction of Jerusalem and the temple.

Conclusion

In the past this passage has led many people to hate Jews. Yet evangelicals today have abandoned the antisemitism of the past and have become some of the strongest supporters of the modern state of Israel. Despite this welcome change, some Christians have continued to maintain persistent negative attitudes toward Jewish people. Too often this is related to their perception that the Jews stand uniquely guilty of the death of Yeshua of Nazareth. Understanding that the phrase "the Jews" in 1 Thessalonians 2:14 refers to the Jewish leaders and not the entire Jewish nation can help halt these negative perceptions of the Jewish people and the idea that the New Testament is inherently antisemitic.

---

38. It might be offensive to some Jewish people to understand the Roman destruction of Jerusalem as judgment for rejecting Yeshua. Recognizing it as such is not done with glee or recrimination. When God chastens his chosen people, it is exceedingly sorrowful in his eyes and in the eyes of those who love him. Furthermore, even the Rabbis, in Shabbat. 119b and Yoma 9b, viewed this catastrophe to be a judgment for national sins (although, of course, they did not include the rejection of Yeshua as one of those sins).

Second Thessalonians

Delay Is Not Denial – Yeshua Will Rescue
All Those Who Wait for Him!

Introduction

Sha'ul is accepted as the author of Second Thessalonians. Some modern scholars reject this claim and ascribe its authorship to an unknown writer.[1] Although the exact date of its composition is unknown, it was written from Corinth.

Its purpose is to clarify and explain the reasons for the evident delay of the Day of the Lord, adding a punch-list of necessary further events before the final apocalyptic scenario could unwind (2 Thess. 2.1–11).[2]

This letter has a remarkable prophetic undercurrent that includes, according to Roetzel, significant prophetic pronouncements of judgment (2 Thess. 1:1–8; 2:1–8).[3]

Apocalyptic themes such as eschatological judgment by fire and its delay (2 Thess. 1:8; 2:7–8), the revelation of the man of lawlessness or sin commonly referred to as the Antichrist (2:3b–12), and the establishment of God's Kingdom (2 Thess. 1:10; 2:14) are also prominent.

Sha'ul closes this letter by instructing his *talmidim* to forsake an undisciplined life (3:6–13). Only those who maintain a disciplined life will be able to remain blameless and be prepared for Yeshua's appearance on the Day of the Lord (3:1–5).

---

1. Gaebelein, *Expositor's Bible Commentary*, 302–303.
2. Fredriksen, Paula. *Paul: The Pagan's Apostle.*
3. Aune, *Prophecy in Early Christianity*, 261.

OUTLINE OF
SECOND THESSALONIANS

I. Salutations and Blessings (1:1–2)

II. The Day of Judgment Will Surely Come (1:3–12)
- A. Thanksgiving for perseverance and trust that withstands persecution and suffering (1:3–4)
- B. God's righteous judgment (1:5–1)
  - 1. Recompense for the Thessalonians (1:5–6)
  - 2. Yeshua revealed with his angels in a fiery flame (1:7)
  - 3. Punishment and eternal destruction (1:8–9)
  - 4. God will glorify His people (10–12)

III. Events That Will Occur Prior to the Coming of the Lord Yeshua (2:1–12)
- A. The Day of the Lord is yet to come (2:1–3a)
- B. The Apostasy must occur (2:3b)
- C. The revelation of the Man of Lawlessness including his false miracles and deceptive practices (2:3c–9)
- D. The self-imposed destruction of those who would not believe the truth because they delight in wickedness (2:10–12)
- E. Thanksgiving for those who have believed the truth (2:13–14)
  - 1. They are the Firstfruits destined for deliverance (2:13)
  - 2. They will receive the glory of the Lord (2:14)
- F. God will comfort those who confidently wait for Yeshua's return (2:15–17)

IV. Concluding Remarks (3:1–18)
- A. Prayer for Sha'ul (3:1–2)
- B. God is faithful to protect his people (3:3–5)
- C. The characteristics of a disciplined life (3:6–15)
- D. Prayer for God's *shalom*
- E. Personal closing

TEXT OF
SECOND THESSALONIANS

1 From: Sha'ul, Sila and Timothy

To: The Messianic Community of the Thessalonians, united with God our Father and the Lord Yeshua the Messiah:

Grace to you and *shalom* from God the Father and the Lord Yeshua the Messiah.

We must keep thanking God for you always, brothers, as is appropriate; because your trust continues to grow greater, and the love you each have for one another continues to increase. Therefore, we boast about you in the congregations of God because of your perseverance and trust in all the persecutions and troubles you are going through. This is clear evidence that God's judgment is just; and as a result, you will be counted worthy of the Kingdom of God for which you are suffering. For it is justice for God to pay back trouble to those who are troubling you, and to give rest along with us to you who are being troubled, when the Lord Yeshua is revealed from heaven with his mighty angels **in a fiery flame. Then he will punish those who don't know God,**[1] that is, those who don't listen to the Good News of our Lord Yeshua and obey it. They will suffer the just penalty of eternal destruction, **far away from the face of the Lord and the glory of his might**.[2] On that Day, when he comes to be glorified by his holy people and admired by all who have trusted, you will be among them, because you trusted our witness to you.

---

1. 2 Thess. 1:8; Isa. 66:15; Jer. 10:25; Ps. 79:6.
2. 2 Thess. 1:9 Isa. 2:10, 19, 21.

With this in view, we always pray for you that our God may make you worthy of his calling and may fulfill by his power every good purpose of yours and every action stemming from your trust. In this way, the name of our Lord Yeshua will be glorified in you, and you in him, in accordance with the grace of our God and the Lord Yeshua the Messiah.

But in connection with the coming of our Lord Yeshua the Messiah and our gathering together to meet him, we ask you, brothers, not to be easily shaken in your thinking or anxious because of a spirit or a spoken message or a letter from us claiming that the Day of the Lord has already come. Don't let anyone deceive you in any way.

For the Day will not come until after the Apostasy has come and the man who separates himself from *Torah* has been revealed, the one destined for doom. He will oppose himself to **everything** that people call a **god** or make an object of worship; **he will put himself above** them all, so that he will sit in the Temple **of God** and proclaim that he himself is **God.** [3]

Don't you remember that when I was still with you, I used to tell you these things? And now you know what is restraining, so that he may be revealed in his own time. For already this separating from *Torah* is at work secretly, but it will be secretly only until he who is restraining is out of the way. Then the one who embodies separation from *Torah* will be revealed, the one whom the Lord Yeshua **will slay with the breath of his mouth** [4] and destroy by the glory of his coming.

When this man who avoids *Torah* comes, the Adversary will give him the power to work all kinds of false miracles, signs, and

---

3. 2 Thessalonians 2:4 Ezekiel 28:2.
4. 2 Thessalonians 2:8 Isaiah 11:4; Job 4:9.

wonders. He will enable him to deceive, in all kinds of wicked ways, those who are headed for destruction because they would not receive the love of the truth that could have saved them. This is why God is causing them to go astray, so that they will believe the Lie. The result will be that all who have not believed the truth, but have taken their pleasure in wickedness, will be condemned. But we must keep thanking God for you always, brothers whom the Lord loves, because God chose you as firstfruits for deliverance by giving you the holiness that has its origin in the Spirit and the faithfulness that has its origin in the truth. He called you to this through our Good News, so that you could have the glory of our Lord Yeshua the Messiah.

Therefore, brothers, stand firm; and hold to the traditions you were taught by us, whether we spoke them or wrote them in a letter. And may our Lord Yeshua the Messiah himself and God our Father, who has loved us and by his grace given us eternal comfort and a good hope, comfort your hearts and strengthen you in every good word and deed.

Finally, brothers, pray for us that the Lord's message may spread rapidly and receive honor, just as it did with you; and that we may be rescued from wicked and evil people, for not everyone has trust. But the Lord is worthy of trust; he will make you firm and guard you from the Evil One. Yes, united with the Lord we are confident about you, that you are doing the things we are telling you to do, and that you will keep on doing them. May the Lord direct your hearts into God's love and the perseverance which the Messiah gives.

Now, in the name of the Lord Yeshua the Messiah we command you, brothers, to stay away from any brother who is leading a life of idleness, a life not in keeping with the tradition you received from us. For you yourselves know how you must imitate us, that we were not idle when we were among you. We did not accept anyone's food without paying; on the contrary, we labored and toiled, day and night, working so as not to be a burden to any of you. It was not that we hadn't the right to be supported, but so that we could make ourselves an example to imitate. For even when we were with you, we gave you this command: if someone won't work, he shouldn't eat! We hear that some of you are leading a life of idleness—not busy working, just busybodies! We command such people—and in union with the Lord Yeshua the Messiah we urge them—to settle down, get to work, and earn their own living. And you brothers who are doing what is good, don't slack off! Furthermore, if anyone does not obey what we are saying in this letter, take note of him and have nothing to do with him, so that he will be ashamed. But don't consider him an enemy; on the contrary, confront him as a brother and try to help him change.

Now may the Lord of *shalom* himself give you *shalom* always in all ways. The Lord be with all of you.

The greeting in my own handwriting: From Sha'ul. This is the mark of genuineness in every letter, this is what my handwriting looks like.

The grace of our Lord Yeshua the Messiah be with you all.

COMMENTARY

1:2. Grace to you and *shalom* from God the Father and the Lord Yeshua the Messiah.

Claudius was the Roman emperor (41–54 C.E.) who was alive during the time Sha'ul wrote to the Thessalonians and was designated by the Roman Senate as *Pater Patriae*, or Father of the Fatherland. His son Nero, who succeeded him in 54 C.E. and may have been emperor during the composition of Second Thessalonians, also received that title.

In the *Tanakh*, God declares himself to be the Father of the children of Israel who is his firstborn son (Exod. 4:22), and in Deuteronomy 32:6 he is called both Father and Creator. God raised and brought up His children (Isa. 1:2), and Isaiah further declares: "But now, *ADONAI*, you are Father; we are the clay, you are our potter: and we are all the work of your hands" (64:7(8)).

God also appears as a Father in the Apocrypha (e.g., Tob. 13.4; 3 Macc. 5.7; Jub. 1.25; Sira 23.1, 4; Wisd. 2.16).[1]

Yeshua instructs his Talmidim "to be perfect, just as your Father in heaven is perfect" (Mt. 5:48). In prayer they are to address God as "Abba," a term of endearment for a father (Mt. 6:9).

As in 1 Thessalonians, Sha'ul's calling God "Father" was saying that though the secular authorities and even the Thessalonians may have considered Caesar to be their father, their true father was God. In the future it is not Caesar who will come and bring permanent *shalom* to their city; it is God the Father who is sending Yeshua to establish the Kingdom of God on the Day of the Lord (5:1–3).

---

1. Lachs, *A Rabbinic Commentary*, 119, 123.

SECOND THESSALONIANS
CHAPTER ONE

1:4–5. Therefore, we boast about you in the congregations of God because of your perseverance and trust in all the persecutions and troubles you are going through. This is clear evidence that God's judgment is just; and as a result, you will be counted worthy of the Kingdom of God for which you are suffering.

Sha'ul presents a prophetic declaration that the Thessalonians' present suffering is an indication that God's judgment is at hand. Persecution and opposition are eschatological signs that they are living during the times of *Chevlai HaMashiach*—the birth-pains of the Messiah (Mt. 24:8–28). After the suffering of those days the Son of Man will appear and gather his elect (Mt. 24:29–31).

1:6–10. For it is justice for God to pay back trouble to those who are troubling you, and to give rest along with us to you who are being troubled, when the Lord Yeshua is revealed from heaven with his mighty angels in a fiery flame. Then he will punish those who don't know God, that is, those who don't listen to the Good News of our Lord Yeshua and obey it. They will suffer the just penalty of eternal destruction, far away from the face of the Lord and the glory of his might.

Sha'ul continues with a midrash on eschatological judgment. Rabbi Daniel Boyarin explains that midrash is a way of contextualizing multiple verses and passages in the Bible, to determine their meaning.[1]

---

1. Daniel Boyarin, *The Jewish Gospels: The Story of the Jewish Christ*, 148–149.

God's throne is described as engulfed with fiery flames "whose wheels were all ablaze. A stream of fire flows from his presence; thousands and thousands minister to him, millions and millions stood before him" (Dan. 7:9–10). Isaiah declares that God will judge the "unrighteous" with fire and sword (66:15–16; cf. Jer. 10:25; Ps. 79:6) and then establish a new heaven and a new earth (Isa. 66:22–24).

In addition, on the Day of Judgment, the unrighteous will try to escape God's judgment by entering cracks in the rocks and holes in the ground but to no avail (Isa. 2:10, 19, 21; Hos. 10:8). Parallel verses can be found in Revelation 6:15–17:

> Then the earth's kings, the rulers, the generals, the rich and the mighty — indeed, everyone, slave and free — hid himself in caves and among the rocks in the mountains, [16] **and said to the mountains and rocks, "Fall on us, and hide us**[a] from the face of the One sitting on the throne and from the fury of the Lamb![17] For the Great Day of their fury has come, and who can stand?"

Destruction of the world by fire is also frequently mentioned in Apocalyptic writings. Some examples include:

> The Sibylline Oracles. There it is said that, at the time of the judgment "a cataract of fire" will pour out of heaven (III. 54); all mankind will be destroyed by "fire upon the earth" (III. 542, cf. II Bar. 27.10; 70.8); "fire and cataclysm of rain" together with "brimstone from heaven" will execute God's terrible judgment (III. 690f.). In Dan. 7.g-IO it is said of the "Ancient of Days" that "his throne was fiery flames" and that "a fiery stream issued and came forth from before him." God's wrath, as a flame of fire, goes forth against sinners (Ps. of Sol. 15.6f.); and the souls of the wicked are tortured in the fires of Hades (Apoc. of Abr. 31, etc.).

1:10–12. On that Day, when he comes to be glorified by his holy people and admired by all who have trusted, you will be among them, because you trusted our witness to you. With this in view, we always pray for you that our God may make you worthy of his calling and may fulfill by his power every good purpose of yours and every action stemming from your trust. In this way, the name of our Lord Yeshua will be glorified in you, and you in him, in accordance with the grace of our God and the Lord Yeshua the Messiah.

Sha'ul encourages the Thessalonians to not lose their confidence in the message he had proclaimed. Those who continue to fight the good fight of faith and patiently wait for Yeshua's return on the Day of the Lord will be glorified by him and have a share in his Kingdom.

SECOND THESSALONIANS CHAPTER TWO

2:1–3a. But in connection with the coming of our Lord Yeshua the Messiah and our gathering together to meet him, we ask you, brothers, not to be easily shaken in your thinking or anxious because of a spirit or a spoken message or a letter from us claiming that the Day of the Lord has already come. Don't let anyone deceive you in any way.

This entire chapter is a midrash on the coming of the Lord based on Daniel 9:27, 11:31–36; 12:11–13 and corollary verses such as Isaiah 11:4; 65–66; Job 4:9.

The Thessalonians had been deceived by an unnamed prophet who had come to Thessaloniki claiming Sha'ul had sent him to inform them that the Day of the Lord had already come. This errant piece of theology shook their faith, like a ship that was "tossed to and fro by the waves and whirled about by every wind."[1]

2:3b–4. For the Day will not come until after the Apostasy has come and the man who separates himself from *Torah* has been revealed, the one destined for doom. He will oppose himself to everything that people call a god or make an object of worship; he will put himself above them all, so that he will sit in the Temple of God and proclaim that he himself is God.

The Apostasy and the man who separates himself from the Torah (Dan. 9:27, 11:31–36; 12:11) had been previously identified as Antiochus IV ("Epiphanes"), who conquered Jerusalem in 167 B.C.E.

---

1. Williams, *Paul's Metaphors*, 74.

and erected an altar to Zeus in the Temple. 1 Maccabees 1:54 and 6:7 refer to this as a fulfillment of Daniel's prophecy. However, Yeshua interpreted these verses as applying not to Antiochus but to the Antichrist that would desecrate the Temple during the Last Days (Mt. 24:15; cf. Dan. 9:27, 11:31–36; 12:11–13).

The specific type of apostasy that would occur before Yeshua's return is yet to be identified, though the text seems to indicate the Thessalonians understood what Sha'ul meant. The Apostasy may be referring to a rejection of the Torah and Jewish traditions for a secular philosophy such as Hellenism, which occurred during the time of the Maccabees, or embracing the religion of the Man of Lawlessness, also called the Man of Sin. Daniel states that the King who has been identified as the Man of Lawlessness will speak against the God of gods. He will have no regard for the God of his fathers and will honor the god of strongholds (Dan. 11:36–38). The Apostasy may also refer to former messianic believers who have abandoned the faith (Mt. 24:11, 12, 24; 1 Tim. 4:1ff; 2 Peter 2:1–22).

Since Greek manuscripts vary, the term in this verse for the Antichrist may appear as the Man of Lawlessness or the Man of Sin. These two terms are synonymous. Since the word for lawlessness as a noun appears in 2:7 and as an adjective in 2:8, the term Man of Lawlessness is preferable.[2] Jewish literature attests to the term Man of Lawlessness.[3] Lawlessness can be defined as referring to a person who is alienated from the Torah through sinful actions, rejects its precepts as binding and/or abandons by implication the God of Israel for foreign gods.

Sha'ul midrashically combines Daniel 11:36–45 and Ezekiel 28:2 where it is stated that a king will elevate himself above

---

2. Gaebelein, *Expositor's Bible Commentary*, 323.
3. David Lincicum, Ruth Sheridan, and Charles M. Stang, *Law and Lawlessness in Early Judaism and Early Christianity*.

everyone, sitting in the Temple and proclaiming himself to be God. This desecration of the Temple by the Antichrist would be the event that would indicate the imminent appearance of Yeshua and the subsequent events that pertained to the Day of the Lord (Mt. 24:15–21). D. S. Russell holds that Ezekiel 38–39 deeply influenced the conception of the Antichrist.[4]

It is interesting to note that Rashi, like Yeshua, interpreted Daniel 9 as referring to the events that would occur at the "End of Days."

> This [Daniel 9] refers to the fate of the Romans—or their inheritors—in the Messianic era. The city will be desolate until the final war (the war of Gog and Magog, as described in Ezekiel 38–39). The leader of the enemy (the Roman emperor) will forge a pact with the Jews for one "week" (i.e., seven years), but for half of this "week," he will disrupt the Temple sacrifices. (With the exception of the daily offering, all other sacrifices were suspended three years prior to the destruction of the Temple because of the siege. And, according to the Talmud in Gittin 56a, the siege lasted three years.) Idols, which are unliving abominations, will be erected in the Temple, until the designated time of its destruction.[5]

2:5–7. Don't you remember that when I was still with you, I used to tell you these things? And now you know what is restraining, so that he may be revealed in his own time. For already this separating from *Torah* is at work secretly, but it will be secretly only until he who is restraining is out of the way.

Sha'ul is surprised that the Thessalonians had become so unsettled by a false prophecy. He was under the impression they had clearly understood his teaching concerning all the details in

---

4. Russell, *The Method & Message*, 191.
5. Rabbi Eric Levy, "Daniel – Chapter 9." *OU Torah*. https://outorah.org/p/3359.

relationship to the Day of the Lord, especially that it could not occur until the public manifestation of the Man of Sin in the Temple. Though the process that would eventually reveal the one who would cause the sacrifice to cease would come (Dan. 9:27), the Restrainer was preventing that from happening. It seems from these verses (2:5–7) that the Thessalonians knew the identity of the one Sha'ul referred to as the Restrainer.

Scholars have not been able to determine definitively or conclusively who or what Sha'ul meant by the "Restrainer." For a variety of reasons, most scholars lean toward the Holy Spirit being the Restrainer. I disagree.

Since context and the similarity of language enables one to grasp the significance of a particular phrase, concept, or event, I have concluded that the Restrainer is God the Father. God the Restrainer restrains or prevents the revelation of the Man of Sin until the Good News about the Kingdom will be announced throughout the entire world as a witness to all the nations (Mt. 24:14). I was pleasantly surprised that Roger D. Aus has come to a similar conclusion: "He who restrains" derives from Isa. 66:9 and is God himself. That which is restrained is integrally related and signifies the will or plan of God that the gospel be proclaimed to all men.[6]

To determine the meaning of the word "restrainer / restraining" and its various forms, I applied one of Hillel's seven hermeneutical principles for interpreting Scripture, which is *Ka-yotze bo mi-makom acher* ("like that in another place"). This principle signifies explaining the meaning of a biblical passage according to another of similar content or language.[7] I also decided to determine if "restrainer" had been used within the context of eschatological

6. Roger D. Aus, "God's Plan and God's Power: Isaiah 66 and the Restraining Factors of 2 Thess. 2:6–7," https://www.jstor.org/stable/pdf/3265992.pdf.
7. *Baraita* of Rabbi Ishmael.

prophecy concerning the End of Days and the Day of the Lord. Isaiah 66 meets these criteria.

The Hebrew word used for restraining, *atzar*, is frequently associated with God's exploits. He restrains Sarah from giving birth (Gen.16:2), the wives and concubines of King Abimelech from giving birth as a punishment for his taking Sarah into his harem (Gen. 20:18), the rain from falling (Deut. 11:17), and plagues from continuing (2 Sam. 24:25). It also refers to restraining a person from acting because he is held in bondage (Deut. 32:36), restraining a person against his will (Judg. 13:15,16), and controlling or restraining a group of people by the king or person who is ruling over them (1 Sam. 9:17).

Atzar (Isa. 66:9), and its Greek equivalent *katecho* (2 Thess. 2:6–7), signifies God preventing *someone* from acting and/or *something* from happening.

In Isaiah 66:9, God *will not* restrain or prevent the restored Jerusalem from giving birth to all her children. These are the children who will be the inhabitants of the New Heavens and the New Earth (Isa. 66:22). The birth of Jerusalem's children will occur prior to the time when God judges the earth with fire (Isa. 66:15–16).

Sha'ul utilizes "restrain," *atzar/atechok*, in a dual sense (2 Thess. 2:6–7). The Restrainer, who is God, is restraining the man of sin in prison, which means "to prevent an evil person or power from breaking out as one imprisons criminals to protect society against them."[8]

Sha'ul draws a parallel between Isaiah 66 and 2 Thessalonians 2:6–7. In the same way that God will not allow anyone from preventing Jerusalem from bearing all her children (66:9), the revelation of the Antichrist and the subsequent Day of the Lord

---

8. Kittel et al., *Theological Dictionary of the New Testament*, 829.

are being delayed/restrained because, in his mercy, God desires that all people will be saved and come to the knowledge of the truth (1 Tim. 2:4).

The delay of judgment and the coming of the *Mashiach* in response to repentance is well-attested in Jewish thought, the prime example being God sparing Nineveh from destruction because they responded to Jonah's message with sincere repentance: "When God saw by their deeds that they had turned from their evil way, he relented and did not bring on them the punishment he had threatened" (Jonah 3:10).

Aryeh Kaplan Z"L[9], a noted rabbinic scholar, writes:

> God will bring the redemption in His own time. If all Israel were to return to God, the Messiah would appear, and the final redemption would be ushered in immediately. Otherwise, the redemption will not occur until the final time decreed by God. This is the meaning of the verse, "I, God, will accelerate it in its due time" (Isaiah 60:22). That is, if Israel is worthy, God will *hasten* the redemption; if they are not, it will come, but only *in its due time*.[10]

The delay of the Day of the Lord had been a problem to the Old Testament prophets (e.g., Hab. 2:2–3) as well as the Qumran community (Habakkuk Commentary 1 Qphab vii. 6-14).[11]

Then *ADONAI* answered me; he said,
"Write down the vision clearly on tablets,
so that even a runner can read it.
For the vision is meant for its appointed time;

---

9. *Z"L* after a person's name means that person is dead. It is an abbreviation for the Hebrew phrase *Zichrono livracha* ("Of Blessed Memory"). The feminine form is *zichronah livracha*. The correct way to pronounce the abbreviation is "zahl."
10. Kaplan, "The Pre-Messianic Era," https://aish.com/48931432.
11. Bo Reicke, *The Epistles of James, Peter and Jude* 179.

it speaks of the end, and it does not lie.
It may take a while but wait for it;
it will surely come, it will not delay."
Habakkuk 2:2–3

Though retribution is approaching, it will not come in the immediate future; but its time is fixed by God.[12]

Kefa (Peter) observes that for God concepts of time are relative.

> The Lord is not slow in keeping his promise, as some people think of slowness; on the contrary, he is patient with you; for it is not his purpose that anyone should be destroyed, but that everyone should turn from his sins.[13] (2 Peter 3:9)

The Thessalonians should be thankful that God's eschatological judgment is delayed in order that all may come to repentance.

2:8. Then the one who embodies separation from *Torah* will be revealed, the one whom the Lord Yeshua will slay with the breath of his mouth and destroy by the glory of his coming.

This verse is a direct reference to Job 4:9 and Isaiah 11:4.

At a breath from God, they perish;
at a blast from his anger, they are consumed.
Job 4:9

But he will judge the impoverished justly;
he will decide fairly for the humble of the land.
He will strike the land with a rod from his mouth
and slay the wicked with a breath from his lips.
Isaiah 11:4

---

12. A. Cohen, *The Twelve Prophets*, 219.
13. Reicke, *The Epistles*, 178.

After the Good News has been proclaimed to the ends of the earth and the birth of the complete number of God's children has been fulfilled, God will no longer restrain the Man of Sin from being revealed. The Thessalonians can be assured that the ultimate destruction of the "one who embodies separation from Torah" (Antichrist) is guaranteed. The Lord Yeshua will slay the Man of Sin with the breath of His mouth and destroy him with the glory of his coming.

2:9–12. When this man who avoids *Torah* comes, the Adversary will give him the power to work all kinds of false miracles, signs, and wonders. He will enable him to deceive, in all kinds of wicked ways, those who are headed for destruction because they would not receive the love of the truth that could have saved them. This is why God is causing them to go astray, so that they will believe the Lie. The result will be that all who have not believed the truth, but have taken their pleasure in wickedness, will be condemned.

When the man who avoids the Torah (the Man of Lawlessness) comes, Satan will give him the power to manifest false miracles, signs and wonders and the ability to further deceive those who are already headed for destruction. His coming is also identified as a *parousia*. However, while the purpose of Yeshua's *parousia* is to establish the Kingdom of Light, the *parousia* of the Man of Lawlessness is to establish the Kingdom of Darkness.

The notion of a "spirit of deceit" sent or implanted by God is known in Jewish theology of this period. The Qumran Rule of the Community explains human behavior because of God's setting within each person "two spirits, one of truth and one of deceit" (1QS III.18–26, esp. 18–19). A "spirit of deceit" (from God?) motif is also common in the Testament of the Twelve Patriarchs (Peerbolte 1996, 88).[14]

---

14. Timothy A. Brookins, *First and Second Thessalonians*, 208.

Those who will not repent and instead take pleasure in wickedness are self-condemned.[15] This idea is expressed in Psalm 81:10–12; Isaiah 64:6(7); and Acts 7:42 (cf. Jer. 19:13; Amos 5:25–32).

Idolatry is a form of apostasy and wickedness that stubbornly resists the will of God. Consequently, God permits idolators to arrogantly follow their heart's fantasies, which leads to their own self-imposed destruction (Ps. 81:10(9)–13(12) (cf. 1 Sam. 15:23).[16]

> "There is not to be with you any foreign god;
> you are not to worship an alien god.
> I am *ADONAI* your God,
> who brought you up from the land of Egypt.
> Open your mouth, and I will fill it."

> "But my people did not listen to my voice;
> Isra'el would have none of me.
> So I gave them over to their stubborn hearts,
> to live by their own plans."
> Psalm 81:10(9)–13(12)

God's children have forsaken their Father's advice, so He leaves them no other alternative but to suffer the consequences of their misdeeds, which is self-inflicted destruction (Isa 64:6(7); cf. Rom. 3:9; 11:32; Gal 3:22).

> No one calls on your name
> or bestirs himself to take hold of you,
> for you have hidden your face from us
> and caused our misdeeds to destroy us.
> Isaiah 64:6(7)

---

15. Le Cornu and Shulam, *A Commentary*, 57.
16. Avrohom Chaim Feuer and Nosson Scherman, *Tehillim Sefer Tehilim: A New Translation With a Commentary Anthologized From Talmudic, Midrashic and Rabbinic Sources*, 1031–1033.

God turns his heart away from those who worship the stars and offer up sacrifices to idols. The idols in the desert during the time of the Exodus included the Ammonite god Moloch, to whom human sacrifices were offered and Rephan, a god of the stars. [17] The consequences of their choice to worship idols was wandering and dying in the wilderness and God withdrawing his promise for that generation from entering the promised land (Acts 7:42, quoting Jer. 19:13 and Amos 5:25–32).

> So God turned away from them and gave them over to worship the stars—as has been written in the book of the prophets. [18]
>
> "People of Isra'el, it was not to me
> that you offered slaughtered animals
> and sacrifices for forty years in the wilderness!" [19]
> Acts 7:42

The theology of Romans 1:20–25 is influenced by the above Scriptures. [20]

> For ever since the creation of the universe his invisible qualities—both his eternal power and his divine nature—have been clearly seen because they can be understood from what he has made. Therefore, they have no excuse; because, although they know who God is, they do not glorify him as God or thank him. On the contrary, they have become futile in their thinking; and their undiscerning hearts have become darkened. Claiming to be wise, they have become fools! In fact, they have exchanged the glory of the immortal God for mere images, like a mortal human being, or like birds, animals, or reptiles!

---

17. Fruchtenbaum, *Ariel's Bible Commentary*, 167.
18. Jer. 19:13.
19. Amos 5:25–27.
20. Shulam and Le Cornu, *A Commentary*, 57–59.

This is why God has given them up to the vileness of their hearts' lusts, to the shameful misuse of each other's bodies. They have exchanged the truth of God for falsehood, by worshipping and serving created things, rather than the Creator—praised be he for ever. *Amen.*

2:13. But we must keep thanking God for you always, brothers whom the Lord loves, because God chose you as firstfruits for deliverance by giving you the holiness that has its origin in the Spirit and the faithfulness that has its origin in the truth.

The word translated "firstfruits" in this verse can be easily misunderstood as it is frequently confused with *Bikkurim,* which includes the firstfruits offering of the wheat harvest that is associated with Shavuot (Deut. 16:1–10; 28:26). The more-accurate translation should be "the firstfruits of the barley harvest" (*omer reisheit kehtzirchem*), a ritual associated with Passover.[21] Judaism does not consider this "first barley-harvest offering" a separate Feast (Lev. 23:9–15) but incorporates it as a specific activity as part of Passover.

There was a difference of opinion as to when the omer of barley was to be presented.

> Leviticus 23 says that the omer of barley should be sacrificed "on the morrow after Shabbat." But it turns out that the interpretation of this passage was a matter of acrimonious disagreement between the rabbis and the members of the sect known as Boethusians. Like the Sadducees, the Boethusians rejected the authority of the rabbis and offered their own interpretations of the Torah, especially on matters of the calendar and Temple rituals.
>
> In this case, they believed that Leviticus should be read, so that the omer would be brought on the day after the first Shabbat after

---

21. Menachem Moshe Oppen, in *The Korban Mincha: A Pictorial Guide to the Korban Mincha,* 40.

the first day of Passover. The rabbis, on the other hand, understood the words "the morrow after Shabbat" to refer not to an ordinary Shabbat—what the rabbis call a "Shabbat of Creation," commemorating God's resting on the seventh day—but simply as a "day of rest," which can also refer to a festival. In this case, they say, it refers to the first day of Passover. This means that the omer is always offered on the same calendar date—the 16th of Nisan, the second day of Passover—and so Shavuot is always on the same date, 50 days later, which is the sixth of Sivan.[22]

The 16th of Nissan then begins a 50-day period of the counting of omer, which culminates on Shavuot with the offering of the two loaves (*shtei halechem*). This counting between these two offerings is known as the *Sefirat Haomer* or the counting of the omer (Lev. 23:15).

Yeshua rose from the dead on the First Day of the week following the first Shabbat after the first day of Passover (Mt. 28:1–10; Mk. 16:1–8; Lk. 24:1–11; Jn. 20:1–30). Since he is the "Firstfruits of the resurrection (firstfruits of the barley harvest)" (1 Cor. 15:20), it is reasonable to assume that his disciples had embraced the Sadducees' interpretation.

Unique among offerings in the Temple, the Omer offering was brought with great fanfare.[23]

> On the day before the festival of Passover, the agents of the court would go out [to the field] and tie [the barley] into bundles while it was still attached to the ground so that it would be easy to reap. On the evening after [the first day of] Passover, all the inhabitants of all the neighboring villages would gather so that it

---

22. Adam Kirsch, "Four Power," *Tablet*, October 23, 2018. https://www.tabletmag.com/sections/belief/articles/daf-yomi-256-flour-power-omer.
23. Rambam, Hilchot Temidin UMusafin 7

would be reaped with much flourish. They would have three men reap three *se'ah* of barley in three baskets with three sickles. ... After reaping, they would bring the barley to the Temple courtyard, where they beat, winnowed, and roasted the kernels over the fire in a cylinder. The kernels were then spread out in the Temple courtyard and the wind wafted through it. The barley was then brought to a mill and ground to produce three *se'ah* (approximately 6.5 gal.), and after it had been sifted with 13 sifters, an *issaron* (one-tenth) was removed.

This *issaron* of fine barley flour was taken and mixed with oil, and a handful of frankincense was placed upon it. It was waved in the eastern portion of the Temple courtyard in all four directions—up, down, right, and left. It was then brought close to the tip of the southwest corner of the altar like the other meal offerings. A handful of the meal was taken and offered on the altar's pyre. The remainder was eaten by the priests like the remainder of all other meal offerings.[24]

The offering of the omer of barley was a sacrifice known as the *Korban Omer*, or "sacrifice of the omer of barley." Its symbolism with Yeshua's sacrifice is clear. The resurrection is compared to the death of a seed that was planted in the ground which springs forth from the earth. The word often translated as "seed of wheat" is a generic term for any kind of grain.

Yes, indeed! I tell you that unless a grain of wheat that falls to the ground dies, it stays just a grain; but if it dies, it produces a big harvest. (John 12:24)

---

24. Yehuda Shurpin, "What Was the Omer Offering (*Korban Ha'omer*)?", https://www.chabad.org/library/article_cdo/aid/4354506/jewish/What-Was-the-Omer-Offering-Korban-Haomer.htm.

Sha'ul writes the following in 1 Corinthians 15:23. The Messiah is the First fruits; then those who belong to the Messiah, at the time of his coming:

Yeshua's death and resurrection is the first fruits harvest, which points to the certainty of a future greater harvest—namely, the resurrection at the time of the *parousia*. Sha'ul reassures the Thessalonians that God has included them in this harvest.

Finally, brothers, pray for us that the Lord's message may spread rapidly and receive honor, just as it did with you; and that we may be rescued from wicked and evil people, for not everyone has trust.

SECOND THESSALONIANS
CHAPTER THREE

3:1a. Finally, brothers

After thoroughly reviewing what he had previously taught the Thessalonians concerning the details about the *parousia* (2:5), Sha'ul switches roles from a Torah teacher to that of a loving father for the purpose of reminding his spiritual children to remember not to forget several important matters. These matters specifically relate to the Thessalonians' life experience as believers in Yeshua.

3:1b–2. Pray for us that the Lord's message may spread rapidly and receive honor, just as it did with you; and that we may be rescued from wicked and evil people, for not everyone has trust.

As believers, the Thessalonians had learned the importance of praying for the welfare of their leaders (Acts 17:1–10) and how personal prayer enables a person to effectively withstand persecution, which, in turn, serves as a witness to the power and truth of the gospel (2:4–5). Prayer opens the door to discernment, which further enables believers to test everything and to judge between good people and those evil people who try to deceive others with false prophecies and misleading teaching (2:2:1–3).

3:3. But the Lord is worthy of trust; he will make you firm and guard you from the Evil One.

The Evil One refers to Satan. He is the father of evil people. Their attacks on the righteous are instigated by their father, the Evil One.

> That the expression "the Evil One" was common in early Rabbinical writings is evidenced from its use in such passages as Midrash Shemot Rabbah c. 21 "God delivered me over to the

Evil One," Midrash Devarim Rabbah c. 11 "the Evil One, the head of all Satanim," and Baba Batra 16a, where Job ix. 24 is quoted "the earth is given into the hands of the Evil One."[1]

3:5. May the Lord direct your hearts into God's love and the perseverance which the Messiah gives.

The phrase "God's love" is a reference to the words of Yeshua (Mk. 12:28–31) that emphasize that the Thessalonians should love God with all one's heart, soul, and strength (Deut. 6:5)[2], which includes loving one's neighbor as oneself (Lev. 19:18).

> One of the *Torah*-teachers came up and heard them engaged in this discussion. Seeing that Yeshua answered them well, he asked him, "Which is the most important *mitzvah* of them all?" Yeshua answered, "The most important is,
>
> **'Sh'ma Yisra'el, ADONAI Eloheinu, ADONAI Echad [Hear, O Isra'el, the LORD our God, the LORD is one], and you are to love ADONAI your God with all your heart, with all your soul,** with all your understanding **and with all your strength.'**
>
> The second is this:
>
> **'You are to love your neighbor as yourself.'**
>
> There is no other *mitzvah* greater than these." (Mark 12:28–31)

3:6–13. Now, in the name of the Lord Yeshua the Messiah, we command you, brothers, to stay away from any brother who is leading a life of idleness, a life not in keeping with the tradition you received from us. For you yourselves know how you must imitate us, that we were not idle when we were among you. We did not accept anyone's food without paying; on the contrary, we labored and toiled, day and night, working so as not to be a burden to any of you. It was

---

1. Lightfoot and Hughes, *Notes on Epistles of St Paul*, 126–127.
2. This verse is a part of the *Shema* (Deut. 4–9) and known as the *V'ahavtah*.

not that we had not the right to be supported, but so that we could make ourselves an example to imitate. For even when we were with you, we gave you this command: if someone won't work, he shouldn't eat! We hear that some of you are leading a life of idleness—not busy working, just busybodies! We command such people—and in union with the Lord Yeshua the Messiah, we urge them—to settle down, get to work, and earn their own living.

Idleness may be a reminder of the men who hung around the marketplace who were hired to persecute and harass the members of the emergent community of believers (Acts 17:5–8). These men are described as idle males who frequent the marketplace who are hucksters and whose idleness leads them into all kinds of trouble. The Greek may correspond to the Hebrew *batlanin*, which represents "idlers" who hang around the marketplace all day not wishing to be employed (cf. Mt. 20:6; Pes. 51b, 55a: Ber. 17b)[3] except for being hired to applaud or heckle anyone according to the desire of those who paid them.[4] Luke further defines these men as evil (cf. 2 Thess. 3:2), indicating that they are quite eager to participate in disturbances.[5]

Sha'ul was not an idle person. He was a hard worker who earned his living in the marketplace as a tent maker.

3:13–15. And you brothers who are doing what is good, do not slack off! Furthermore, if anyone does not obey what we are saying in this letter, take note of him and have nothing to do with him, so that he will be ashamed. But do not consider him an enemy; on the contrary, confront him as a brother and try to help him change.

Sha'ul commends the Thessalonians for doing what is good—their acts of loving-kindness (*gemilut chasidim*). He emphatically

---

3. Le Cornu and Shulam, *A Commentary*, 931.
4. Fruchtenbaum, *Ariel's Bible Commentary*, 360.
5. Le Cornu and Shulam, *A Commentary*, 932.

warns those who are idle to heed his instructions to be gainfully employed. The people who "who hang around the marketplace all day not wishing to be employed" should be ostracized by the community for the purpose of motivating them to get a job.

3:17.   The greeting is my own handwriting

It is likely that Sha'ul dictated his letters to an amanuensis, probably Silas.[6] A personal "greeting" like the one here occurs at the conclusion of 1 Corinthians (16:21), Galatians (6:11), Colossians (4:18) and Philemon (v. 19), where Sha'ul makes a concluding reference to his "own hand."

> A reference to one's own handwriting at the closing of a letter was not unusual in the ancient world. Since many people wrote through an amanuensis, including those among the literate and highly educated (Klauck 2006, 55), the sender often took the pen in closing (Klauck 2006, 16, 138). This need not have been for the purpose of authentication. Rather, there was something in the very handwriting that brought the sender nearer, as it provided "real traces, real marks, of an absent friend" (Seneca, Ep. 40.1; cf. Chariton, Chaer. 8.4.5–6).[7]

On the other hand, Sha'ul may have needed to authenticate this letter because previously an unknown person purporting to be his designated representative had come to Thessaloniki and had deceived them with a false prophecy or written document.

---

6. Lightfoot and Hughes, *Notes On Epistles of St Paul*, 135.
7. Brookins, *First and Second Thessalonians*, 230.

SELECTIVE BIBLIOGRAPHY

Aune, David Edward. *Prophecy in Early Christianity and the Ancient Mediterranean World*. Grand Rapids: Eerdmans, 1991.

Aus, Roger D. "God's Plan and God's Power: Isaiah 66 and the Restraining Factors of 2 Thess. 6–7." *JBL* 96, 1977. https://www.jstor.org/stable/pdf/3265992.pdf.

Bockmuehl, Markus. "1 Thessalonians 2:14–16 and the Church in Jerusalem." *Tyndale Bulletin*, May 1, 2001. https://doi.org/10.53751/001c.30258.

Bockmuehl, Markus. *Revelation and Mystery in Ancient Judaism and Pauline Christianity*. Grand Rapids: Eerdmans, 1997.

Boyarin, Daniel. *The Jewish Gospels: The Story of the Jewish Christ*. New York: New Press, 2012.

Bradshaw, Robert. "The Purposes Behind Paul's First Epistle to the Thessalonians." January 1, 1990. https://www.biblicalstudies.org.uk/article_1thess.html.

Brookins, Timothy A. *First and Second Thessalonians*. Grand Rapids: Baker, 2021.

Burke, Trevor J. *Family Matters: A Socio-Historical Study of Kinship Metaphors in 1 Thessalonians*. London: T&T Clark International, 2003.

Cohen, A. *The Twelve Prophets*. London: Soncino, 1977.

Cook, Michael J. *Modern Jews Engage the New Testament: Enhancing Jewish Well-Being in a Christian Environment*. Woodstock, VT: Jewish Lights, 2009.

Davies, W. D. *Jewish and Pauline Studies*. London: SPCK, 1984.

Dickieson, Brenton. "Antisemitism and the Judaistic Paul: A Study of 1 Thess. 2:14–16 in Light of Paul's Social and Rhetorical Contexts and the Contemporary Question of Antisemitism." 2006. https://www.academia.edu/4033038.

Flusser, David. *Judaism and the Origins of Christianity*. Jerusalem: Magnes, 1988.

Fredriksen, Paula, and Adele Reinhartz. *Jesus, Judaism, and Christian Anti-Judaism: Reading the New Testament After the Holocaust*. Louisville, KY: Westminster John Knox, 2002.

Fruchtenbaum, Arnold G. *Ariel's Bible Commentary: The Book of Acts*. San Antonio: Ariel Ministries, 2020.

Gaebelein, Frank Ely. *The Expositor's Bible Commentary: Volume 11: Ephesians Through Philemon*. Grand Rapids: Zondervan, 1978.

Gilliard, Frank D. "The Problem of the Antisemitic Comma Between 1 Thessalonians 2.14 and 15." Cambridge Core, *New Testament Studies* 35.4, February 5, 2009. https://www.cambridge.org/core/journals/new-testament-studies/article/abs/problem-of-the-antisemitic-comma-between-1-thessalonians-214-and-15/BFD57B5732D7590FE827B4FD747031A8.

Gruber, Yeshaya. "Can a Comma Be Antisemitic?" *Israel Bible Center*, July 27, 2023. https://weekly.israelbiblecenter.com/can-a-comma-be-antisemitic.

Ishai-Rosenboim, Daniella. "Is יום ה (the Day of the Lord) a Term in Biblical Language?" *Biblica* 87.3, 2006. https://www.jstor.org/stable/42614691.

Kacenberg, Mala. *Mala's Cat*. New York: Pegasus, 2022.

Keener, Craig S. *A Commentary on the Gospel of Matthew*. Grand Rapids: Eerdmans, 2005.

Keener, Craig S. *Acts: An Exegetical Commentary*. Grand Rapids: Baker, 2012.

Kittel, Gerhard, et al. *Theological Dictionary of the New Testament*. Grand Rapids: Eerdmans, 1985.

Koelner, Yosef, and Jeffrey Seif. Sha'ul/Paul – *God's Shaliach's (Apostle) Corresponds with the Corinthians – 1 Corinthians – Restoring a Congregation in Crisis – 2 Corinthians – Countering Messianic Madness*. Clarksville, MD: Lederer, 2023.

Koelner, Yosef. *Cosmic Warfare; The Final Destruction of Amalek by the Messianic King*. Plantation, FL: Yeshivat Rabban Gamaliel, 2023.

Koelner, Yosef. *Paul's Letter to Titus: His Emissary to Crete – About Congregational Life*. Clarksville, MD: Lederer, 2022.

Lachs, Samuel Tobias. *A Rabbinic Commentary on the New Testament: The Gospels of Matthew, Mark, and Luke*. Hoboken: KTAV, 1987.

Lash, Jamie. *The Ancient Jewish Wedding: And the Return of Messiah for His Bride*. Ft. Lauderdale: Jewish Jewels, 1997.

Le Cornu, Hilary, and Joseph Shulam. *A Commentary on the Jewish Roots of Acts*. Jerusalem: Netivyah Bible Instruction Ministry, 2003.

Levine, Amy-Jill. *Jewish Annotated New Testament*. Oxford University Press, 2017.

Levinskaya, Irina. *The Book of Acts in Its First Century Setting*. Grand Rapids: Eerdmans, 1996.

Lightfoot, J. B., and E. Selwyn Hughes. *Notes on Epistles of St Paul from Unpublished Commentaries*. London: Macmillan, 1895.

Maimonides, Moses, and Eliyahu Touger. *Mishneh Torah*. New York: Moznaim, 1987.

Marshall, I. Howard, and Karl P. Donfried. *New Testament Theology: The Theology of the Shorter Pauline Letters*. Cambridge University Press, 2010.

Neusner, Jacob. *Judaism in the Beginning of Christianity*. Philadelphia: Fortress, 1984.

Reicke, Bo. *The Epistles of James, Peter, and Jude*. Garden City, NY: Doubleday, 1985.

Riesner, Rainer, and Doug Stott. *Paul's Early Period: Chronology, Mission Strategy, Theology*. Grand Rapids: Eerdmans, 1998.

Russell, D. S. *The Method and Message of Jewish Apocalyptic: 200 B.C. – A.D. 100* Philadelphia: Westminster, 1984.

Rydelnik, Michael, and Michael G. Vanlaningham. *The Moody Bible Commentary*. Chicago: Moody, 2014.

Rydelnik, Michael A. "Was Paul Anti-Semitic? Revisiting 1 Thessalonians 2:14–16." *Galaxie*, Winter 2023, https://www.galaxie.com/article/bsac165-657-06.

Sanders, E. P. *Jewish Law from Jesus to The Mishnah: Five Studies.* London: SCM, 1990.

Sanders, E. P. *Paul, the Law, and the Jewish People.* Minneapolis: Fortress, 1985.

Silver, Abba Hillel. *Messianic Speculation in Israel.* New York: Macmillan, 1927.

Slotki, I. W., and A. J. Rosenberg. *Isaiah: Hebrew Text & English Translation.* New York: Soncino, 1987.

Stern, David H. *Jewish New Testament Commentary: A Companion Volume to the Jewish New Testament.* Clarksville, MD: Jewish New Testament Publications, 1999.

Stone, Michael Edward. *Jewish Writings of the Second Temple Period: Apocrypha, Pseudepigrapha, Qumran Sectarian Writings, Philo, Josephus.* Assen: Van Gorcum, 1984.

Vermès, Géza. *Jesus the Jew: A Historian's Reading of the Gospels.* Philadelphia: Fortress, 1988.

Weiss, Meir. "The Origin of the 'Day of the Lord' – Reconsidered." *Hebrew Union College Annual*, Vol. 37, 1966. https://www.jstor.org/stable/23503114.

Williams, David J. *Paul's Metaphors: Their Context and Character.* Peabody, MA: Hendrickson, 1999.

Printed in the United States
by Baker & Taylor Publisher Services